THE LOVE AND POWER OF GOD

Missionary Experiences In The Jungles of Ecuador

Maria Luisa Jimenez Edwards

Gotham Books

30 N Gould St.
Ste. 20820, Sheridan, WY 82801
https://gothambooksinc.com/

Phone: 1 (307) 464-7800

© 2023 *Maria Luisa Jimenez Edwards*. All rights reserved.

No part of this book may be reproduced, stored in a retrieval system, or transmitted by any means without the written permission of the author.

Published by Gotham Books (August 3, 2023)

ISBN: 979-8-88775-412-3 (P)
ISBN: 979-8-88775-413-0 (E)

Because of the dynamic nature of the Internet, any web addresses or links contained in this book may have changed since publication and may no longer be valid.

The views expressed in this work are solely those of the author and do not necessarily reflect the views of the publisher, and the publisher hereby disclaims any responsibility for them.

*Selected real life experiences
In the jungles of Ecuador,
South America.*

Table of Contents

Acknowledgments v

Author's Notes vii

Chapter 1

My Childhood Desire to be a Missionary 1

Chapter 2

The Good News in Lago Agrio 15

Chapter 3

Perspective from the Vicar 25

Chapter 4

Life In a Native Quechua Community 39

Chapter 5

Monsignor the Good Shepherd 55

Chapter 6

The Life Cycle From Birth To Death 69

Chapter 7

Living in Christian Unity 83

Chapter 8

A New Group From and For The Mission 109

Chapter 9
Living Out Our Commitment For The Poor 129

Chapter 10
The Women Find Their Power 147

Chapter 11
At Last, Our Very Own Home 163

Chapter 12
Walking with the Poor 183

Chapter 13
The Earthquake 197

Chapter 14
Growing Pains and Moving On 213

Acknowledgments

This work is a testimony of my journey, as a missionary, immersing me, in the lives of the wonderful people I meant along the way. Many stand out and deserve acknowledgement and my profound gratitude. First and foremost, I give God all glory and honor and praise because without Him I would not have had these experiences.

My parents, Julio Cesar and Rosario Jiménez have always been so rich in love. Education and good work ethics were especially valued by my dad. My mother succeeded because she lived what she taught, both spiritually and morally. She taught us that love, happiness, and success are with God's help within everyone's reach, if you really want to attain them. I want to thank my family (Aurelio, Fabiola, Germania, Nila, Mercedes, Ricardo, Celso, Virgilio, and Nelly) who loved and supported me through this journey. They specifically assisted me in bringing the good news of Christ to, my beloved people of Ecuador.

I would especially like to thank Bishop Gonzalo Lopez Maranon who accepted me, encourage me, and gave me the responsibilities I had in the mission field. Many friends challenged me to write this book.

To all of my friends especially to: Rosa, who may be smiling from heaven, Doctor Kindle, Louise, Reverend Supancheck and the Sisters of St. Joseph of Orange, who generously granted me the scholarship to G.T.U. Berkley.

I am also grateful to the participants in the communities, and particularly the young people who helped start the group COIM. I so appreciated Elida, Inez, Mary, Gladys, Carmen, Mery Sadia and those who joined us later. We labored together preparing and setting the foundations for what is COIM in the Sucumbíos Church (the church in

Ecuador.) I feel honored to have become a part of their lives; because of their unreserved effort, through much affliction and joy. During those eight years on the mission field, they have been eternally fixed in my heart. May God in His abundant love and generosity bless, protect, and care for them all. I am forever grateful for sharing our journey.

There are many people who provided invaluable assistance in completing this project. I am so thankful for them; to my husband Dan Edwards, for his support, to Donita my sister-in- law, to Mary Katherine, and Nancy my new friend, who played a great part in editing this book.

Author's Notes

As a child I desired to be a missionary. It held an indescribable allure for me, an intrinsic pull that was aching to spread the Good News of Jesus. In the pages of this book, join me, as we embark on a personal and spiritually-challenging journey to the jungles of Ecuador.

The ideals I presented to the people are for me, as well as, for them. But as you read "Please be patient. God is not finished with me yet." It is virtually impossible to describe a missionary life meaningfully, to someone who has never experienced it. I want to encourage the readers to find their own path to follow God, as others, in the midst of utmost poverty have found.

As I wrote these stories I was encouraged anew. I challenge all of you to acknowledge your talents and move forward with your dream. Your opportunity is as wide as your vision. My heart repeats the words of the Psalmist, *"What can I ever give to the Lord in return for all the things which he has given to me?"* My response is my love and praise forever.

Thank you, my Lord.

Maria Luisa Jiménez Edwards

Chapter 1

My Childhood Desire to be a Missionary

*"For I know well the plans I have in mind for you
Says the Lord, plans for your welfare, not for woe! Plans to give you a future full of hope."*

Jeremiah 29: 11 (TNAB)

The first missionary I ever met was Reverend Tramarollo in 1948. He was from Italy. I was about four years old. He stayed at my parents' home. He lived with us because there was no house for the Priest yet. I was born in Borja, Ecuador, South America. When I was able to understand and talk freely, I asked the Priest how he could leave his mother and father and come to us. As I remembered, he explained that he wanted every one of us to Know God. He wanted us to know about the tremendous love God has for all of us, and that God wants all to know of His love.

The priest moved into his place when the town's people and my father finished the construction. The priest continued to come to our home for meals. He had many stories to tell! The seed for being a missionary was planted in me during those early years.

Our town grew and when I was thirteen the missionaries gave me a scholarship to study far away in Tena, Napo Province. Mercedes, my younger sister, also received a scholarship from the city of Baéza. We were sent to a missionary boarding school to study and came back home only in the summer time.

I accompanied the priest, during summer vacation, wherever he went helping to teach of Jesus. I loved working with the children because of their eagerness to learn about God. The children and I enjoyed the time we had together. I also appreciated the opportunity to ride on the missionaries' horses, which were the best in the area.

While in my last year of college in Ecuador, I met a lay missionary, Julia. She was teaching English at the college. We became friends. She asked me what I wanted to do after graduation; I let her know of my desire to be a missionary. However; I did not like the Sisters who were teaching me.

"What is it you do not like about these Sisters?" She asked.

"Well, there is racial prejudice among them, and I believe it is not right." I could see that all the European Sisters were called Mothers (Madres) and were teachers or had important administrative jobs.

The ones born in Ecuador were the Sisters (Hermanas), which meant they did all the cleaning, cooking, answering the door, taking care of the animals, boarding school needs, and any other menial work, but they were not teaching or given the opportunity to further their studies.

Julia immediately said to me, "I know of a community in the United States where everyone is a Sister. There is no difference between them, and I know you will like them." I thought this would be a better situation. Nevertheless, they were too far away, to even think about joining them. I wanted to be a missionary in my own country. Julia responded, "What if I told you it would be possible for you to go there to be trained, and then come back to be a missionary here?"

I thought about it. English was not my favorite subject. Besides, I would have to leave my family.

We had no money for such trips. She saw my hesitation and guessed what I was thinking.

She continued." I know the Sisters very well and they will find a way. Why don't we pray and wait? I will write to them." I forgot about that conversation until I received a letter in Spanish from Sister Yolanda of the Society Devoted to the Sacred Heart in California (SDSH). I was very surprised, happy and confused at the same time.

I went to my closest friends and read the letter to them. Everyone had advice on what to do. We were a close group of six, including my younger sister Mercedes. Some of my friends thought the letter was a joke. I could not possibly become a religious Sister. They knew me well, after living together in the boarding school for six years. Others suggested that I should respond to the letter and see where it went.

Another thought it would be a good chance for me to go to the States, and take advantage of the chance to find a rich strong, blue eyed guy and then come back to Ecuador. We had fun with that letter.

After thinking a little more, I wrote her and to my surprise, Sister Yolanda answered right away. We continued corresponding. She described the community ministries I would be expected to do. I took my first employment after college was as a third grade teacher. I worked in the Catholic Mission School in Cotundo, Ecuador, and continued to pray about going to the USA. The school was a boarding school for aboriginal boys and girls. The boys and girls lived in separate buildings. At that time, I met a teacher who wanted to marry me as soon as possible. He said he was so much in love with me. The feeling was not mutual. I continued my correspondence with Sister Yolanda.

I taught for one year in that mission school. Then I transferred to a public school (better pay) in the town of Ponce Loma, Ecuador. I taught first, second and third grade.

The first graders spoke only Quechua, and came to class naked. That was a very eye opening experience which I never forgot.

Sister Yolanda, wrote to me and invited me to visit SDSH.

My response was, "I thank you for your gesture but I have neither money nor intentions to go to the United States." She wrote that the Sisters were planning on going as missionaries to South America. This would be a good opportunity for me to see if I liked missionary work. I would be trained and sent back to Ecuador as a missionary. This way they would fulfill their goal. They would pay my plane fare and suggested I bring my guitar.

My father did not want to hear about it. He wanted me to continue helping him finance the education of my younger brother Celso. I had already helped him one year. It was difficult for me to know what to do.

Mercedes, my younger sister, came to my rescue and told me. "If you really want to go, I will help educate Celso." She was already helping Virgilio, my other younger brother. She wanted me to have the opportunity to be a Sister. Then I would be free to go and follow my dream. For this I am ever grateful to her.

I answered the Sisters that I would accept their invitation to go to the United States. I would be trained and come back as a missionary to my people.

In January 1967, I arrived in the U.S.A. where I was welcomed by the Sisters at the airport. The whole picture was so different from what I had expected; nothing like what I was used to. Everything was so big, the airport, the many cars, the beautiful tall buildings, houses, gardens and all in abundance.

I was assigned to live in a convent in East Los Angeles at Our Lady of Lourdes Parish. Sister Yolanda was the Superior. This was to see if I liked the life of a Sister before I started the official training. Sister Aurelia, one of the founders, was a European Sister from Hungary who also lived in that convent along with Sister Catherine, Sister Elaine, and Sister Cathleen from the USA.

The Sisters sent me to adult night school to learn English. While attending these classes I met a Peruvian young man who became very interested in me. He wanted to be my boyfriend but, of course, I let him know why I was there.

While getting to know the life, place, and customs of the Sisters, I was able to give Catechetical classes for the Spanish-speaking children and youth, mostly from Mexico. I had the opportunity to teach Spanish to the Pastor/Abbot, Benedictine monk Rev. Nathe. He was my first Spanish language student in the U.S.A. of Our Lady of Lourdes Parish. He wanted to be able to speak Spanish, to communicate with the people he served. He ministered in a totally Hispanic area. He was smart and had a gift for languages. He was practicing with the people who came to the rectory for help. They were delighted to hear him try to understand them. We became good friends and kept contact. I started the training in the SDSH.

As a Sister, I worked with children, youth and adults in pastoral work in many parishes, as a Catechetical teacher, visiting families, giving Bible classes, and parenting classes. I did it all because in my heart, I wanted to learn everything in order to go back to Ecuador. I loved to teach the young. Their desire to know Jesus was most inspiring for me. They were like sponges soaking up the message.

While in California, one of the things I enjoyed the most was to be able to take food and clothes to the poor in East Los

Angeles. I was living in the Wilshire area close to Hollywood. The people from the farmers market gave whatever produce they could not sell to the Sisters, instead of throwing it away. The Sisters took the produce to the poor. During my training years, we went regularly with a station wagon to get the food, clean the vegetables, put them in boxes and deliver them.

I worked in Orange, Santa Ana Parish and Our Lady of Guadalupe: Mission Santa Inez in Solvang, Buellton, Santa Maria, and Los Olivos. For a couple of years, I was part of a team giving summer Bible classes in Oregon. Other summers I worked in Reno, Nevada.

I received many gifts from the people I worked with one I especially remember was from members of "Guadalupanas group" in Buellton, California. For my final vows they gave me a ring, an expression of their appreciation for my work with them and for making a positive difference in their lives. It was of deep significance in my commitment to God and to His people.

After fifteen years with SDSH, there was no sign of a plan for any of us Sisters to go to the mission field. Catholic Religious Communities have what we call *Chapters* to revise the Constitution of a Community if necessary. Some have it every five years, or according to the needs. Representatives from different convents in different states would attend this very important event.

At the general chapter of the SDSH Community in 1979, while revising the constitution, the word "missions" was almost deleted. I spoke strongly against this deletion and would not let go of it, because Sister Yolanda in the name of the SDSH community had told me they were missionaries.

I left my country, Ecuador to learn how to be a missionary. I wanted to bring the Good News about the Kingdom to

Ecuador and to Gods' people, at the far ends of the earth. After much deliberation and discussion, one small phrase was left: "We will also evangelize in the mission places."

After that, my hope of ever going to be a missionary started to dwindle away. I talked to my spiritual director. He suggested asking for a year of experience working with missionaries to see if that was what I really wanted to do with my life.

I ask the Superior General and founder of SDSH to send me but she denied my request. I again, after six months wrote to the General Council reminding them of my reason for coming to the States and becoming a Sister. It was to return to Ecuador as a missionary. I had the letter they had written promising me the training I needed to fulfill that promise. I felt ready to go. The Council answered: "If you want to go, you go on your own. Do not count on us." This was devastating for me. I did not understand. With one stroke of the pen I was cut off from everyone who had become my new family for fifteen years. However, I took it knowing that God had a plan for my future.

I strongly believed that God convicted me and I was going to follow His lead. They bought me a ticket to Quito, Ecuador and gave me $175 in cash.

From the money I received I was able to get some pencils, candy for the children in my family, some socks, handkerchiefs and hairpins as a token memory of my life in the States. In my culture, when you return to Ecuador, you do not come empty handed.

Many times, talking to God, I would ask, "Why I am not like the other Sisters, content and happy with whatever is asked of them? Why do I want more? Why do I think you want more of me?" The answer was, "I love you."

I prayed over and over the following Psalm was my consolation:

> *Hear my voice Lord, when I call;*
> *Have mercy on me and answer me,*
> *"Come" says my heart, "seek God's face,"*
> *Your face, Lord, do I seek!"*
> *Do not hide your face from me,*
> *You are my help; do not cast me off;*
> *Do not forsake me. God my savior!*
> *Even if my father and my mother forsake me,*
> *the Lord will take me in.*
>
> Psalm 27: 7-8(TNAB)

God was on my side; I had strength which I knew could only come from Him, and peace in knowing I was doing what I was convicted to do. I left behind very dear friends and 15 years of devoted service. I felt alone and stripped of everything familiar. I thought how Jesus must have felt when he was stripped of his clothes and nailed to the Cross. However, the Resurrection was in sight and that for me was definitely a source of encouragement. I decided to start anew.

At that time, I was in charge of the whole program of Religious Education in Resurrection Parish in East Los Angeles. We had classes from Kindergarten through High School. One of the activities was a teacher training course where we had a good group.

When word got out about my leaving, the teachers called the Catholic newspaper "Tidings," printed an article saying I was leaving for the mission field. The Parish gave me a "going-away party," but I was not able to attend. The teachers taped with their thoughts and best wishes and Reverend Norm brought it to me. He was always a good friend. Before I left a friend Mary took me, to a restaurant for a steak dinner and said, "Who knows if it will be the last steak meal you have?" She was so right.

The plane took me to Quito, Ecuador. During the 15 hour flight, I had a lot of time to pray and to think of the turn my life had taken. I prayed many Psalms; the ones I knew by heart, especially the 23 Psalm.

The Lord is my shepherd;
There is nothing I lack.
In green pastures you let me graze;
To safe waters you lead me;
You restore my strength.
You guide me along the right path
for the sake of your name.
Even when I walk through a dark valley,
I fear no harm for you are at my side;
your rod and staff give me courage.
You set a table before me as my enemies watch;
You anoint my head with oil;
my cup overflows
Only goodness and love will pursue me
all the days of my life;
I will dwell in the house of the Lord for years to come.

Psalm 23 (TNAB)

I repeated this Psalm over and over again. I had mixed feelings; the excitement in seeing my family again and to be able to follow my dream. Everyone was gathered at my sister Mercedes' home to welcome me. After the cake, I began telling them what had happened and why I had come back to stay.

I planned to follow my dream. My brothers suggested that I needed to see and talk to the Cardinal.

The very next day I went and talked to Cardinal Vega and I told my story. He listened patiently and then he said he had a proposition for me. "You came right at the time of need. God has sent you here. The official visit of the Pope in Rome is coming up and I need a report of all the work of evangelization we are doing in the country, specifically in the Diocese here in Quito. You will visit every parish and get the statistics of what is going on. I will take that report to Rome. After that we will see where you can serve the Lord best. I will have you in my prayers. I am sure God will let us know." He also told me I would receive token money for bus fare and for my services.

With such an offer, I felt a strong sense of peace. Again my family would help me find a central place to stay, so that my traveling by bus would be easier. Gladys my brother sister in-law had a spare room, so I went to live north of Quito in St. Charles neighborhood with their family.

Now Psalm 27:1-3(TNAB) came to my mind and from that day on it was my daily prayer:

> *The Lord is my light and my salvation,*
> *Whom do I fear?*
> *The Lord is my life's refuge;*
> *of whom am I afraid?*

This was clearly an answer from God. The highest official authority of the Catholic Church in Ecuador put me to work immediately. I was being prepared for the next step. Because of that job I was able to get to know how evangelization was done in Ecuador. I met many wonderful people of all lifestyles. Very generous people were helping as volunteers in the parishes in different ministries. I met the Catholic school principals and teachers. It was a grand opportunity given to me.

After three months, I presented the report to the Cardinal. He was delighted and said, "It is more than what I expected. Now I have been thinking about your future destination and have been asking around. There are two Dioceses in the country that work in the line of Liberation Theology. They take to heart the documents of Vatican II, Medellin, and Puebla.

One is the Diocese in Riobamba with Monsignor Proaño. He ministers specifically to the natives of the high mountains. The other Diocese is to the East in the jungle Lago Agrio with Monsignor Gonzalo Lopez Maranon, a Carmelite."

He gave me the choice of either one. He assured me they would be delighted to have me. I just knew the answer; I did not need time to think. I chose Lago Agrio, the Carmelite Mission. The Cardinal thanked me for the report, wished me luck and gave me the telephone number of Monsignor Gonzalo. He blessed me and I left encouraged.

I felt I knew exactly where God wanted me. The next step was to call and see Monsignor Gonzalo, which was not easy because he often traveled between Quito and Lago Agrio." At that time, he was in Lago Agrio. I had to wait until he came back to Quito. His secretary gave me a possible date to call for a visit with him.

My first impression when I met Monsignor Gonzalo was, "This is a man of God." I felt at peace. He has that gift of making people feel at ease.

He was very jovial, relaxed, and most of all I was surprised he was not wearing the Bishop's robes. He wore ordinary pants and shirt, no clergy collar either. He exuded peace and friendliness.

I liked him immediately. He asked me, "What brings you here from the great USA?" I talked with him for several hours.

He asked a Sister to bring refreshments and kept asking many questions about me personally, the community and my ministries in the U.S.A. I went through my whole story, a repeat of what I had shared with Cardinal Vega.

Monsignor Gonzalo responded, "Splendid." He was very excited that I chose the Carmelite Mission. He eagerly let me know that there are many changes of great importance going on at this time. "It is a time of growth," he said. "The tenth Assembly of the Carmelite Missionaries was celebrated with a special twist. For the first time the Assembly of Missionaries was celebrated in Lago Agrio on April 1980, not in the Sierra. Second, there was a change in the structure of how to run the Assembly. The first three days we spent in a Spiritual Retreat. At the end we finished with a great community Celebration of Reconciliation. The primary subject was, 'The local church.'[1]

His interest and concern was to promote the incorporation of national elements into the board of directors. He explained some history of the Carmelite Order in Sucumbíos and the great efforts towards a change and a new direction his vision was: The option for the poor.

He inspired me by how he knew each missionary, their area of ministry and their spiritual lives. I had not expected that. It was obvious, this shepherd knew his sheep. I did not take notes, and had to try to absorb and remember everything he was saying. It was a vivid memory and later on I wrote my notes about the visit.

Monsignor gave me the information to get to Lago Agrio. When he was not there Reverend Camarero the Vicar gave me an orientation, and showed me what was going on there. Monsignor Gonzalo planned to let the missionaries know about my arrival. He said, "You are the answer to my prayers."

I was amazed and grateful to God I had found my place. My ideals seemed to fit perfectly with the needs of the Carmelite Mission. It was God's timing, I was certain. I left with a great sense of peace that passes all understanding.

On my way to my Sister Mercedes' home, where I was staying at this time, I had the opportunity to reflect on recent events and how my life was unfolding. Psalm 139 kept coming to my mind, and the Song "My life is in your hands."

After a couple of days, I went to the airport to get information about flights to Lago Agrio. I prepared myself with my family's help. I would be closer to them, but still it was hard to say good-bye to my family. They had been supportive and helpful during the time of my searching. I was sure that they all would continue to support me. My main interest was to do God's Will and I felt clearly this was what God wanted of me at this time.

Chapter 2

The Good News in Lago Agrio

"The harvest is abundant, but the laborers are few."

Matt. 9:37(TNAB)

After a long interview with the Bishop, he assured me the missionaries would be delighted to have me join their team. Since it was my first time in the area, I was excited and skeptical at the same time. I only knew in general terms that Texaco was drilling for oil in that area. Since I knew the missionaries only by name, the Bishop had given me a general description of each one who worked there. He had emphasized especially the spirit of the missionaries, their love of God and the people. They were totally surrendered to God's will, and dedicated to spreading the kingdom of God.

My airplane left Quito, Ecuador's capitol, on Wednesday, November 14, 1980. As I looked through the window of the plane, the blue sky was full of white clouds without even the smallest hint of rain. The plane was going eastward and as time passed, I noticed the people on my flight were mostly business people and some regular flyers.

I had plenty of time to reflect on what might lay ahead, the drastic turn my life had taken. I wondered what the future held in store for me. As we were getting closer, as far as the eye could see, there was a vast lush green jungle. When the plane flew over the road, I could occasionally see a very small house; like a forgotten toy here and there by the side of the road with no cities or towns nearby. Around the houses, banana trees and coffee plants could be seen. My heart was pounding at the thought of this adventure that I was taking, and I prayed, "God, it is your will I am trying to follow; I know you are with me." I remembered and repeated the words of the book of Joshua:

> *"Be strong and of good courage;*
> *Do not be afraid, nor be dismayed,*
> *For the Lord your God is with you*
> *Wherever you go."*
>
> *Joshua 1:9. (TNAB)*

At the same time, I felt a great amount of peace, knowing that the fulfillment of my dreams, which God had been preparing me for the last fifteen years, had finally come.

My dream was to be a missionary like one of those I had met in my early childhood, the kind Italian Josephine's Priest and the Doroteas Sisters. I saw how kind and dedicated they were. They helped the people learn more of Jesus and they spread the Kingdom of God's Love.

It took about 90 minutes to reach Lago Agrio, a booming city in the middle of a jungle with roads leading in all directions to oil wells. Texaco was the number one company there, plus subsidiaries that came to find the black gold. I had no idea how much work was being done in the jungle by these companies.

To my great surprise, the airport was only a narrow runway in the middle of the jungle. I could see nothing but a forest with huge trees and small and rich vegetation. As the plane landed the full reality of my decision was beginning to dawn on me. My thoughts and prayer continued: "Oh God, I am afraid. Where have I come? Give me the strength to follow your will." The words of God to Abraham came to my mind.

"Do not be afraid; I am your shield, your exceedingly great reward."

Genesis 15:1 (TNAB)

I kept looking but could see nothing familiar. It was like watching a movie but it was real life now. The Airport Administration building was a cement slab with four pillars holding up a roof. At one of the corners was a small closet with no windows. We exited the plane and walked about 90 feet down the runway to where there was a line of people waiting for us to disembark so they could start boarding.

As I turned back, I noticed the plane had never stopped its engines and the people in line were already starting to board. Our bags arrived and the attendants dropped them onto the cement floor. Chaos was all around me with human noise and people moving quickly. It was an organized chaos because everyone seemed to know what to do, except me. We gathered our bags as the plane took off. A woman observed me looking around.

I said, "How can I get to the Carmelite Mission? I need to go there. I see no taxis." The woman answered. "You need to climb into any truck available to go anywhere. The city is a couple of miles away. The open trucks are the taxis.

Some people smiled at me and passed by. The passengers were running with their luggage to take a "taxi" that might still be available. I saw how people climbed into the back of the truck with no problem. I was wearing a brown knee-length dress that was not suited for the occasion. I followed and did the same as everyone else was doing, requesting the driver to take me to the Carmelite Mission.

The open truck had no seats in the back and nothing secure to hold on to. The luggage was thrown in and piled up, in the middle, of the bed of the truck. Everyone had to sit around the bags and hold on to the sides. Men, women, and children seemed to be used to traveling this way. (See picture #1)

When the taxi drove over ditches in the road, I almost fell out of the truck a couple of times. A lady next to me whispered, "You have to hold on tightly if you don't want to fall. I have seen people fall and the driver does not even realize it." I thanked her graciously and held on tightly as she had suggested. My lessons were coming from every direction, but I was ready and willing to learn. It was a very hot and muggy afternoon.

The short distance to the mission road was full of banana trees, birds of paradise, sugar cane, tropical fruit and flowers. When the taxi stopped to let me out at the mission center, another surprise awaited me. No one was around! My arms and buttocks were sore from holding tightly to the side of the truck and the rough ride. The driver indicated that the building in front was the mission center. Another passenger helped me get my luggage down which consisted of a small suitcase, and my guitar.

It was terribly hot, maybe 110 degrees or more and the humidity was about 98% for sure. I had come from a cold-weather city, in the high mountains of the Andes. The heat was a shock to my system. In the short distance I walked, the excitement of it all made me perspire and I became soaking wet. I dropped my belongings at one of the open huts in front of the house and started to look around. Eventually I found the cook and she was surprised to see me there. I introduced myself and told her who I was. Her name was Blanca and she went to find the Priest.

The Bishop had told me about the radio being the Missions' only means of communication. He would let the missionaries know what time I would be arriving, as soon as I let him know what day I would be traveling. There were two times in the day, one in the morning and one in the evening that we could communicate with the different mission centers. After my meeting with him, communication had stopped for a couple of days. The Bishop had been unable to let them know of our arrangements, for me to join the team of missionaries. That explained why no one met me at the airport or at the home.

The Carmelita Mission of Sucumbíos was named after the Carmelite order that had been serving the people for decades. The Priest and Brothers were originally from Spain, and the Carmelite Sisters were from Colombia. As news of the arrival of a new missionary spread, one by one, those who were close by came from their places of work to meet and welcome me. Each one apologized for not knowing about my arrival and said, "We usually go to the airport to welcome newcomers. We know it is a different and difficult experience just to land in the jungle."

They expressed how happy they were to have me there and congratulated me that I had made it so well. The spirit of the group was fantastic as they radiated joy, love, peace and understanding. After their apologies were expressed they went back to their activities promising to meet again at dinner time. My arrival was an important event for the mission. Not often is a new member added to the team. I was given a cold drink of water and then I related my traveling experiences and first impressions. This had to be repeated as I met each one of the missionaries.

Sister Leonila, one of the Carmelite Sisters, volunteered to conduct the "grand tour" of the place where I would live for the time being. She was most gracious and welcoming; she had a great sense of humor. I felt accepted right away. Five

Carmelite Sisters lived in the house. Sister Rita was in charge of the girls in the boarding school, Sister Carmen was a Registered Nurse for the clinic at Lago Agrio, Sister Stella was a nurse for the Communities, and Sister Flor who later on became one of the groups at the local church.

They had a spare room where I would be staying. A couple of feet away from the dorms of the Sisters was another building which houses the kitchen, dining room, and a large room where the mechanic and electrician for the college lived. Behind the kitchen was a big open cement slab for washing clothes and restrooms. About 90 feet from the guest house, was a two story building. This was the boarding/living quarters for teenage girls who were studying at the mission. Another 60 feet further was a building for young men. On the sides of both buildings were bathrooms and showers.

One more block up and around the top of the hill to the west were three buildings where the bishop and other staff lived. In one of them lived the caretaker Mr. Abram with his family; his wife Aurora, a son Santiago 6 years old, and Anna a four month old girl who was premature and not too healthy.

Farther on was another beautiful open space with a hexagon building for conferences, which was able to hold about one hundred people. It had big open spaces for windows and doors.

It was to become the educational center for the people of the area, especially for the farmers. All around there were exotic flowers and colorful tropical bushes. I was excited. It was beyond my expectations. It was awesome. I could not stop thanking God. Finally, I was going to be part of a group who had dedicated themselves to spread the Kingdom of God. Here I was in the Amazon jungle, the country of my birth.

Soon it was time for dinner and all the missionaries not on duty came to eat. There were always some missionaries on duty taking care of the young men and women. After dinner, we gathered to talk in front of the house. Two straw round huts where there with seats providing a place for gatherings. There we could talk and relax after dinner and watch the sunset in the west, when it was not raining. The huts were right in front of the river and the view was spectacular.

The evening was beautiful with moonlight spilling over the river, bringing a tremendous peace. The breeze carried its own perfume, from the Aguarico River. It serenely flowed in front of the mission center.

The running river could be heard from where we were. It sounded like music to our ears, canopied by the stars and palm fronds. I had definitely arrived into another world. The most beautiful sunset I had ever experienced was right in front of me, and it was breathtaking. I could not stop saying how beautiful it was and thanking God for it.

One of the missionaries agreed with me, but added, "Don't forget Maria Luisa, no one lives only on the beauty. There is much more that goes with this." Later on, I would remember these words and reflect on the truth of what was said.

At the evening gathering, everyone wanted to know what made me want to go into missions, and why did I come all the way from United States? I shared my story about what the missionaries had done in my home town of Borja, in my early impressionable childhood. It was then that I had decided to become a missionary. Questions went back and forth from the missionaries because we all wanted to know about each other. Time just flew as we talked under a full moon.

I had many questions as well: Why were they here? What made them come as missionaries from Spain and Colombia? They had left their countries and families to be here. At that time only one of the missionaries, a Priest, was a native from Ecuador. The missionaries were from different places yet we had so much in common. We had the same goals and reasons for being in the Amazon Jungle. Their answers gave me more affirmation to my own reasons for being there: "We are fools for Christ."

They told me of the great need for missionaries, especially local ones, and reminded me that, "The harvest is great but the laborers are few." We finally went to bed with the promise to make time to keep sharing and getting to know one another. Soon plans would be made for the post at which I would work.

My first night at the mission I could not sleep. I was thinking of the day and how my life had been transformed by the jungle beauty. The night animal noises from the jungle, kept me awake for a long time. My goal was clear and finally. I was going to be able to experience what I had so longed and prepared for.

I started my journaling. I wrote about my arrival at Lago Agrio. I prayed in thanksgiving for the day, the safe trip and just being there. It seemed like a dream. Many Psalms came to my mind, and I recited them all especially:

The heavens declare the glory of God and the firmament shows His handy work.

Psalms 19:1 (TNAB)

Each Psalm meant so much to me now. Every word I was savoring, praising and talking to my God. After a long time and with great peace, I fell into God's arms and slept. God's plan was being unfolded for me. The circumstances of how I had come were not as I had dreamed. I spent my last fifteen years preparing to work in the Community. During that time I was an instrument of God growing spiritually strong to go though whatever I needed to go through. I did not have financial backing nor spiritual and emotional support. It was me and my God. That was enough for me. My faith was put to the test, and here I was.

We have a saying, "God writes straight, even with crooked lines."

God was writing with this crooked line (me). All I had gone through was worth it. I left everything in God's hands and as always, He was faithful and full of surprises.

Chapter 3

Perspective from the Vicar

"But sanctify Christ as the Lord God in your hearts. Always be ready to give an explanation to anyone who asks you for a reason for your hope."

1 Peter 3:15 (TNAB)

Early the next morning, sunlight fell fresh and brilliant over my bed. My mind gently floated to the surface, and I noticed some small inconsequential things. The simplicity of my room went along with the spirit of the mission. It had a single bed with a mattress over the springs. It was unbelievably comfortable. There was a place to hang clothes in the corner and a cross on the wall over the head of the bed. The glass windows were secured with iron rods, allowing the bright morning light to come through but with no screens. The birds were happily singing their different melodious tunes outside the window. Dogs were barking a short distance away. The warmth of the sheet that lay on top of me was uncomfortable, as I awoke in this new place.

I heard unfamiliar noises and did not remember the trip or my arrival at this house, right away.

I tried to recapture the day before, including last evening's events, and conversations. Most of all I wanted to get orientated and consciously be where I needed to be. My prayer was, "Here I am Lord. I came to do your will." As I continued to get ready for the day, I heard the bell ring for morning community prayers. The building had a chapel where we prayed together using the Common Book of Prayer.

We sang the Psalms of the day, as well as, songs of praise and thanksgiving. We read the message for the day from the Word of God and prayed for the needs of the world, the government, the mission, missionaries and families. Everyone prayed spontaneously and it took longer than usual. At this time, it took on a different and more profound meaning: The daily prayer was from *Luke 1:46-55 (TNAB)* The first verse says:...

"My soul proclaims the greatness of the Lord, my spirit rejoices in God my Savior for he has looked with favor on his lowly servant."

When the time of prayer ended, the bell rang letting everyone know that breakfast was ready. Blanca, the cook, spoke Spanish and had been trained by the Colombian Sisters and knew how to cook very well.

There was small talk about the night before, and everyone wished me a good day of orientation and then all went to their waiting ministries.

Before orientation planned for the middle of the morning, the Vicar Reverend Camarero allowed me to soak in the surroundings at a slow pace. I could better appreciate the details I had missed the day before. The building where I was and would be living was a duplex. One portion in front was the sleeping quarters of the Carmelite Sisters, along with a parlor and a chapel. The building behind had a large room with four beds military style, a kitchen, a dining room behind the kitchen, bathrooms and showers. On the side was a building for washing and hanging clothes to dry in a covered open space. This would be a big enough area to accommodate the youth encounters, because there was no other place, as yet.

Down the hill was a narrow path made by the daily steps of people walking on it. There was a small chicken coup enclosed with wire, for the hens to lay eggs. The little chicks were safe there from the night animals that would happily eat them. The rest of the area was tropical jungle.

The time came to meet with Reverend Camarero, the vicar for the mission. In the Bishop's absence, he made the decisions. He knew about my joining the missionaries. He was very happy to have me there as the need for missionaries was great.

I had a notebook with me to take notes of what I was getting into. "The harvest is great but the laborers are few," he said, repeating the words of Jesus. "We have been praying to the Lord to send us more laborers to take care of God's people in this area. You are the answer to our many prayers." This comment made me feel welcomed, needed and accepted. He gave me a general rundown of the mission; its goals and the way it was working. He told me, "We are here to evangelize, train leaders, and move on to other towns where there is no one to bring the Good News."

Reverend Camarero took a map to point out centers where missionaries are located. They traveled from there to many other communities around.

(See picture #2) They were Puerto del Carmen near the border of Peru, Palma Roja on the shores of the San Miguel de Sucumbíos River, El Playon in the high mountains, close to the border of Colombia, La Bonita, Lago Agrio, Lumbaqui and Tarapoa.

Reverend Camarero shared more information about the specific mission work. "In addition to evangelization, we educate people and care for the sick. We have an elementary school, high school, college and a clinic," he said. "The best way for you to learn is by experience. You will have time to get to know all the ministries we have and see where you would like to minister."

For a couple of months, I was to accompany each one of the missionaries to the different Communities. I was ready and anxious to start getting to know the people I would work with. Those to whom I would minister, challenging them to grow spiritually as the Word illuminated their lives.

The mission was divided geographically into areas: Via Tarapoa, Via Quito, Via San Miguel and Via Coca. Each area had many communities with a team for each one. The communities were a great distance from each other and the vicar explained that our mode of transportation would depend on where we were going. Some places we would have to walk to. That could take an entire day. One could see trails where horses and people had traveled. To other places we would take a bus. To the people who lived by the river, we would travel by canoe. If there was a road, we would use the mission car. He asked me if I knew how to drive.

"Yes" in the city," I responded.

He laughed and made some jokes about my answer to his question saying, "That will be a plus." I had seen the road on my way from the airport. I would need to learn how to avoid the ditches.

At that time, none of the other women at the mission center could drive. I was told that I would be called on to drive regularly. That way, the Brothers and the Priest would be freed for other activities.

Mostly, I would be driving Sister Leonila who was in charge of shopping for food and other needs. This would allow me to learn how to shop, as well as meet the business people with whom we worked, which was quite an art.

He explained over and over again that the best way to get to know each missionary on the team would be to shadow them and see little by little where it would be the most advantageous for me to help. I agreed to any other suggestions he made, including getting familiar with the territory, the people and their needs but most of all, how to evangelize.

There were other teams, and we met with them once a month or according to the needs that arose. It was important to keep communication open and to share our experiences which seemed to have a lot in common. As time passed, I found out just how true this statement was.

Reverend Camarero had more questions about my personal ideas and work before I joined the missionaries. I briefly let him know about my convent life (that is another book in itself) and my desire to be a missionary which had been evident to me even as a small child.

I told him how I worked in the United States, which was primarily in the poor areas with Hispanic people (the majority from Mexico), some from Central America, and a few from South America or Ecuador. In one of the parishes, I was a Pastoral Associate and worked with three communities, the English (white), the Hispanics, and the Filipino (English and Tagalo).

The next question was: "What did you to evangelize?"

I told him that we taught religion, trained teachers, had youth groups youth camps, family camps, as well as visiting families of the parish according to their needs. The work I enjoyed the most was, to visit and take care of the needs of the poor. East Los Angeles was the place where I would take food and clothes to the poor after visiting the families in need. It was our pastoral work evangelizing the people.

"The different needs will call for different approaches and methodology," he said I agreed with him, that understanding a person's culture was very important in the work I had done.

I expressed the belief that my training was adequate and up to date. I planned to continue studying in the understanding and the knowledge of God, His people, and the World. We did pastoral work in many parishes, we taught in schools, and we had a doctor working in a hospital. I visited the families, taught Religion, Bible studies, Parenting, Counseling, children, youth, couples or families, and tried to meet any other need as part of the evangelization. I was trying to keep my explanation brief, but said, "You can ask for more information anytime."

He then said he wanted to hear about my family. "Well that is going to take some time," I responded. He assured me he had all the time in the world, so I proceeded to relate the facts about my family.

I was born in Borja, Canton Quijos, Napo Province one of 10 children. My parents Julio and Rosario Jiménez were originally from El Carchi north of Ecuador, near Colombia. My oldest brother Aurelio and his wife Ana Vinueza live in Archidona, with their five children.

My sister Fabiola lives in Borja with her five young children. She lost her husband in an accident helping the Bishop (his uncle). My sister Germania is a housewife with nine children and lives in Quito with her husband. My sister Nila is not married and lives in Borja taking care of my parents. My sister Mercedes is a teacher who has one son Krystian. Ricardo is married to Guadalupe. They have three boys.

The Vicar heard about my two brothers, Celso who was a teacher in Putumayo is married to Julia has two beautiful girls. Virgilio taught in a school on the road from Lago Agrio to Quito, is married to Esperanza, and they have two children.

Nelly the youngest also lives in Quito.

One more time he wanted to hear why I had chosen to leave the U.S.A. to return to Ecuador to be a missionary (he took notes.) I explained that ever since I could remember, I wanted to be a missionary.

I was impressed by the sacrifices I had seen in other missionaries had made to leave his family for the love of God. Also when I was a third grader when some Sisters came, I remembered thinking that if people from other countries came to help us to know God, surely I should be willing to help my own people.

Reverend Camarero wanted to know where my talents, gifts and passions lay in order to help me decide where I would be best fitted in the work of spreading God's Kingdom. I appreciated his concern and interest and his taking time to get to know me which emphasized that we were really one in Christ. We are His body. If one hurts, all of us hurt. We must truly care for each one as we are precious to God and to one another. He talked of his own vocation and God's call to him, about his family and country of birth, Spain.

According to the vicar, it was expected that the missionary goes to a community about once a month. Each time a visit would be made by two missionaries, which could last one day, three days, a week or more if necessary.

We would be building "Base Christian Communities." He explained what that was, and how we go about building them. The method would have four stages, with each one necessary as the four legs of a table.

1. Observe and listen. (Discuss the community needs.)

2. Judge, In the light of the God's Word. Discuss.

3. Act on it according to the Word of God.

4. Evaluate and celebrate. On the next missionary visit, we would evaluate and celebrate our successes, review our failures, and learned from them. Ask what does God want us to do as an individual and as a community to improve our lives.

As circumstances change, and lives change, we would have to observe the reality as it unfolded with God's Word in our hearts guiding our hands. I knew the subjects; the Gospel, our Catholic Faith, Religion, but this method was another way of spreading God's Kingdom that was not familiar to me, but it made sense.

He emphasized that we needed to empower the people with whom we worked, to do whatever it took to solve their own problems. We would support them with our presence and encouragement.

I was overwhelmed with the abundant amount of material to grasp all at once. For me *"It was a new way of being a missionary and bringing the Kingdom of God to His people.*

He repeated. "We evangelize while they are evangelizing us." I needed to think about this concept. (Being evangelized by those I was evangelizing.) He further explained that as we go to each community, we will offer to help them and in return we would let them provide whatever they could; such as a place to stay, food to eat or anything they had to help us in return. We would be willing to do whatever they needed done whether it was building their home, or planting crops such as coffee, bananas, yucca, or fishing, wash clothes, or clean.

We would be willing wash clothes, or do cleaning. When they show an interest and ask why we are doing such a thing, then is the time to share the gospel of Jesus Christ. It is our new way to teach by modeling. Not just preach but teach as Jesus did by example and with parables stories. Jesus ate and fished, talked and taught the apostles. My response to that was, "Wow."

Usually the Priest or Brother worked with the men, and with the Sisters the women and children. The missionaries did not preach or teach until the people started asking questions, such as: "Why do you do this for us? You know we cannot pay for your work." That indicated they were ready to listen to the Word of God and take part in building the Basic Christian Community. Our job was to prepare the soil for planting the living seed of the Word of God.

"They devoted themselves to the teaching of the apostles and to the communal life, to the breaking of the bread and to the prayers. All who believed were together and had all things in common, and the Lord added to their numbers those who were being saved."

Acts 2:4-44 (TNAB)

This scripture was our goal. Reverend Camarero said, "As we get to know the individual, we can invite them and their families to attend the evening weekly meetings of the Word at the community center." When a missionary visited a community, a meeting would be scheduled for every evening. The community would name a leader as an elder; one whom they felt had the qualities to continue sharing God's word.

We would explain to the leaders what to do as we trained them. After they finished their training at the Mission Center they were called, "Animators or guides of the Community." As the Priest and Sister had done, the leaders would follow the same process.

By the end of the meeting with the Vicar, I was extremely excited about the Bishop's vision. There was much to learn and the process was already in place. I felt supported and thankful to have the opportunity and means to make my dream come true. The long day's orientation ended. However, there was still the possibility of a change when the Bishop came from Quito.

My first ministry

The next day I was sent to the closest community across the Aguarico River, with Reverend Castro. He was a young priest who came from Spain right after his ordination. He was trying to learn the culture while he acquired life experiences. It was a delight to work with him because of his humility, enthusiasm, dedication and energy. (See picture #3)

He reminded me of the Biblical Philip because of what Jesus said about him, "There is a man in whom there is no guile." He was a prayerful dedicated young man who loved his vocation of following Jesus in poverty, while he ministered to the people as an ordained Priest. He said, "I owe my vocation to my mother and grandmother who knew before I was born, that I was going to be a baby boy and a priest."

It was an honor to work with him. His intelligence, coupled with his meekness, gentleness and compassion made him a wholesome person who was extremely effective. Any time he celebrated Mass, we were all truly encountering God.

On one occasion we were crossing a stream that became a rushing river. Across it lay a single log which we had to cross to get to the community. My heart was pounding and I was afraid of falling into the water. I asked for his hand. To my great surprise, he dropped his backpack and found a stick about three or four feet long and an inch wide. He expected me to hold onto one end while he held onto the other. He did not want to hold my hand. I did not understand. I thought it was peculiar.

Much later, I figured out that he was an ordained priest. A young man and young woman together could present the possibility of starting something. In my culture in Ecuador, holding a hand is not a big deal.

Another time we went together to minister to a community. On our way back, it rained so much that we were soaking wet. We made it to the car after a very long walk but we needed to change clothes. Reverend Gabriel very calmly said, "I will change in the car. When Sister Estella came with me, she used to go behind that tree." He pointed in the direction of a big tree quite a way off."

I said, "Well, you can change clothes in the car. I will turn around facing the other way. When you are through, would you please go to the main road where it branches into a Y and watch out to make sure no one comes this way." It was some 90 to 100 feet from where the car was. I was able to change clothes without fighting the ants, snakes and any other little animals in the brush.

Sister Estella had shared her experiences with me about some of the tricks the Priests and Brothers played on her. Thanks to her, I was ready and when we arrived home, I let her know my first experience. Sister Estella had the reputation of being a liberated Sister, and that is why some of the missionaries teased her the most. The worst part of it was that she kept on falling for their tricks, and had many stories to share.

For instance, on one of the trips, nature called after so many hours of walking. Estella told the Priest and Brother who were accompanying her that she was going behind a tree. When she came out, they were gone; she had to continue by herself on a rough jungle path to the home where they would spend the night.

After walking for some time she saw the home across a pasture. There were cows in the very direction she was going. She was afraid of cows; she had to find another way. She was feeling so tired. Estella felt she cannot make it another step. She forced herself to continue on and decided to walk just outside of the barbed-wire fence to stay away from the fearsome cows.

When she arrived at the home and told the lady of the house why she took so long, (the priest and Brother had arrived over an hour earlier) the lady sent her four-year-old son to move the cows to another pasture. He did so by getting a little stick and whoosh the cows away. They immediately obeyed him. Estella felt humiliated because of her fear. Oh how we laughed when she told that story.

On another visit when Estella had to go to the bathroom in the woods, she did it over a bush full of chiggers. (These bugs are so tiny only a near-sighted person can see them. They cause a terrible itch on your skin.) The chiggers were happy to find a feast on her behind.

Since she was a nurse, she carried medical supplies. She put a whole bottle of mercurochrome on the place to stop the itching. The lady of the house quietly whispered, "Sister you have blood on your back side." She said "Oh no! She responded, "Oh yes! Estella told her about the chiggers and the mercurochrome the lady offered to wash her slacks.

Estella said, "I have no other clothes to wear." The lady said, "I will let you borrow my skirt." The only problem was, she was a very short lady and Estella was quite tall. When Estella came out to dinner, the Priest and the Brother could not believe Estella in a mini-skirt. She did not know which way to place her long legs. The embarrassment she felt was beyond words. She had never worn anything above her ankle.

Shopping In Lago Agrio

My first shopping experience in Lago Agrio was unforgettable. I drove Sister Leonila and saw how people loved her very much. Sister Leonila had a charisma when talking to them. She made them feel good and important. I was amazed to see how this Sister bargained with everyone and for everything she never paid the original price. (See picture #4)

With my personality, I could not see me being able to do what she did. She buttered them up so much. Whoever was helping her, she addressed them as "my king," or "my gentleman," "my savior, my lord." That was how she treated them so everyone loved her.

In one of the stories she shared with me, she told of an unforgettable experience which taught her a valuable lesson.

She said; "I started smelling something awful and I had no idea what it was. Even after I took a shower and made sure I did a good job of checking all my clothes, the odor did not disappear. I even put on some baby powder and bought some cheap perfume to wear. All this time the odor got worse, and it was with me wherever I went. I was totally embarrassed and afraid to get close to anyone lest I would offend them.

"One day I decided I had to find the source of this terrible smell. I started with my bed, then my clothes, and any belongings I had. Finally I cleaned out my purse. To my surprise, I found the culprit. I had forgotten the butcher had given me a special steak for me and I had put it in my purse.

It was totally rotten and covered with maggots."

Having learned her lesson she added, "I will never accept anything for myself again. I will put it in the general shopping bag." We were laughing so hard we could hardly talk.

I learned so much from her. Not only how to do the shopping, but how to treat people. Of course, I could never get myself to call anyone "My king" or any such a thing. I had so much to look forward to. Everything was new. I love freshness. It brings a new light, a new life, and sometimes death to old ways and ideas.

Chapter 4

Life In a Native Quechua Community

"All authority has been given to Me, in heaven and on earth. Go therefore and make disciples of all the nations, baptizing them in the name of the Father and of the Son and of the Holy Spirit, teaching them to observe all things that I have commanded you; and know I am with you always, even to the end of the age."

Mathew 28:18-19 (TNAB)

I was sent to visit another part of the mission territory, to keep the above command, with another culture and language. One of the leaders came to accompany me to his Commune. We started early in the morning. For the first part of the trip, we took a bus as far as the road went. Then we carried our back packs and walked. Silently I followed him, trying to keep up to his pace. Once in while he would turn back to see if I was behind him, and would slow down or keep going without one word. I felt secure accompanying him.

It was daytime but it seemed dark because of the many enormous old trees overhead. Occasionally I could see the blue sky or white puffy clouds, threatening a rain. I heard different birds singing their magnificent happy tunes.

The breeze was delightful, as it was hot in that area. Our leader was carrying a long, hollow stick called *"Fucuna,"* his hunting weapon. At times, he would look up and point to a bird or a monkey and blow a poison dart through it. Then, I understood why he walked in silence; it was in case he had the opportunity to kill a bird or a surprised animal.

After a couple of hours on the way to our destination, we went by a big house and I thought we had arrived. He took me in, but there was no one around. "This is my family home," he said. I saw it was empty; just a big open space inside. He read my mind saying, "We moved to a place where there are more people and where we would have some neighbors. We have a couple of hours more to walk before we get there." We rested a couple of minutes. I took the opportunity to find a bush. We continued walking on a less traveled trail. I was getting tired after six hours of walking.

I had my backpack which contained a sleeping bag, a change of clothes and a toothbrush.

I learned the hard way after my first experience, that I must travel light. I had to carry only what I needed for myself. One time, at the beginning, when I visited another community, I almost did not make it. I took too many unnecessary things and after two hours, I was very tired. I had to ask for help to carry my belongings.

We arrived at the house when the sun was almost down. The whole family was there waiting. He said, "Here is my family," and he introduced me to each one of them. "We will stay here." I shook hands with the men, women and children.

The woman of the house brought me their drink called, "*chicha.*" I was very thirsty. We had been walking almost all day without food or water. I had not stopped for fear I would get too far behind and get lost. I had heard about this drink but I had not yet seen the process it took to make it. I drank happily and gratefully. Everybody was watching me and when I finished the drink, they all clapped.

The special drink

Making *"Chicha" is t*he job of the old women of the commune. The women get together in a hut made for this activity. They cook a lot of the long root of the "yucca" (In the potato family but tastes differently). The women sit in a circle close to a large clay pot which is in the middle of the circle. Each woman has a pot of cooked yucca by her side. She chews the yucca and spits it into the big container. It is quite a full-time job. Most of them have few to no teeth. Only very trusted people get to see how they make this drink. It is a secret kept from outsiders.

As time went by, they started to know and trust me better; they let me be a part of this process. When the chewing is finished, they add some sweet potatoes to it. They covered the pot tightly with banana leaves and leave it to ferment gradually causing it bubble. After it has brewed awhile, they start drinking it. The longer it ferments the stronger is the alcohol content and people can get drunk on it.

Some people have changed the practice of how they prepare their drink "*chicha*" by smashing it with a piece of wood (like mashed potatoes) without letting it ferment. It tastes a bit different. When they serve it, they take the liquid from the top. However, at times some pulp from the bottom moves and there are small pieces of yucca, which requires some chewing. It tastes good.

In this area, the walls and floors of the houses are made out of (guadúa which is like bamboo), which allows the air in. The thick bamboo which can be as large as eight inches around, is first slashed with many small lacerations of three or four inches, and when the whole bamboo is slit, then one long cut is made from top to bottom to open it out for a nice piece of building material. When it is finished it is called "chilla."

They cover the roof with interwoven palm leaves. In some areas, they use "*chonta*," a type of palm which is plentiful. The trunk is very valuable and stronger material that lasts longer than chilla. It is harder to work with chonta than with the bamboo.

They build the houses about five feet off the ground for safety from the night animals and from flooding or mud when it rains. It also helps to keep it cool in the summer. I saw that it was very practical.

In the evening, we sat around the fire and the father started talking. I imagined it was about the trip. Occasionally they would look at me and laugh. I laughed with them not knowing about what.

They cooked fresh fish by wrapping them in a banana leaf and placing them on the hole prepared under the fire. Everyone eats from the center pot what they want without using plates or utensils. We sat around the cooked yucca and green banana pot and the unwrapped cooked fish.

I felt honored when they asked me to join in. It meant I was welcome and already trusted as part of the family. Otherwise, they would have given me a piece of banana leaf with some of the food on it apart from their gathering. When the dinner was finished, there were not many dishes to wash, just a couple of big pots. The women took them to the creek, washed them and brought water in for the next meal.

Afterward, the children played in front of the house with a homemade soccer ball made of old rags and twigs. The men looked like they were preparing sticks for the next morning's fishing. The women were weaving new baskets. I decided I would join the children. Some already spoke Spanish well and we could converse a little bit and ask some questions. I began by asking them, "What did you do today?" They told me, "We went fishing for dinner with our mothers because dad went to bring the missionary."

I asked the children, "Do you like to sing?" Unanimously they said "Yes."

"Would you sing for me?" they said, "Yes."

I listened to their singing and then it was my turn to sing. They liked my song and wanted to learn a song. I taught them, "Jesus, Jesus," in Spanish. My Quechua was very poor. I knew a couple of words, not enough to converse.

Soon the chickens started climbing the trees to roost, people started to yawn, and the father told the children to go into the house.

I realized it was time to go to bed. I took my toothbrush and went to the creek to brush my teeth and found a bush for a bathroom. Some children followed me. They sat by the shore of the creek and watched me brush my teeth and wash up.

When they saw I was looking for a bush, they disappeared to give me privacy. They also brushed their teeth with their finger, spit the water out and that was that! I was very tired after a whole day of walking in the jungle. There was much to thank God for (and I did) and went to sleep.

At dawn, I heard the noise of pots and pans, and I could hear the crackling of the fire. It was still dark outside. I woke up slowly. My whole body ached. Every bone that touched the bamboo floor hurt and let me know about it. It must have been four or five in the morning. I heard the father talking. He talked and talked it sounded like monotonous preaching. This went on until the father said, "We are going to eat now."

I got out of the sleeping bag and rolled it up. The children followed me to the creek where I washed up and brushed my teeth.

It was a repeat of the ceremony of the night before including finding the bush.

When I came back to the house, the food was pretty much the same as the night before, fresh boiled green bananas with salt, yucca and fish, but there was also a big teapot full of boiling "*Guayusa*" which we all drank. Guayusa is a leaf that people gather and dry for the regular daily morning tea. There is a legend and a song telling what the Quechua believe, that if you drink the Guayusa tea, you for sure will come back to the place.

After breakfast, about six o'clock in the morning, the women and children went to plant yucca. I went with them. Each woman had a small machete. The machete was used for cutting the weeds (or whatever was there) to clear a place where the yucca was going to be planted. When the plot was cleared they made rows of small holes with a stick, about 3 feet apart, not straight but slanted. They push the yucca stick in to the holes, and piled a bit of dirt around it and went to the next place to plant. I watched them and learned how to do the same.

They did it as a graceful dance. It did not seem like hard work for them. They had many laughs at different times as they watched me clumsily do what they did.

The men disappeared to their hunting duties. The children also had responsibilities. Each had a piece of land which they were planting and were proud when it was finished. They looked at the sun to check the time of day. The woman wanted me to see the other places where they had planted yucca and bananas before. It was a small walk away. The yucca plants were at different stages of growth. In some places, the leaves were barely coming up. In others, they were already full of green leaves. The next ones were mature enough to take and cook. The women dug up some yucca for lunch and we all carried them back home.

The men came with green bananas on their shoulders. The women cooked green bananas and yucca again. This time they brought out dried meat. I had no idea what kind of animal it was, and I wasn't going to ask; it was good.

In the afternoon, we all went to the river. A little walk away from the house, the children and I swam and had so much fun I could have stayed all the rest of the days, happily enjoying my time there. The funny part was that at the same time we were swimming, they told me they were fishing. I saw the mothers and fathers were fishing down the river. The children said, "We are also fishing." I asked, "How?"

They said; "We send the fish that way," pointing to where their parents were silently following the fish. Therefore, I was fishing with them too. "I like this way of fishing," I thought.

Again, I was able to see how everyone in the family does their part and knows their responsibilities. They talk very little. I did a lot of observing. They knew exactly what the other person needed or thought, because at times, what I wished for was already supplied before I said anything. They observe and use body language and facial expressions in silence. I was learning by living with them what I had heard and read about their way of life.

The only clothes they had were what they were wearing. They did not take them off. They swam in them, put soap on the clothes to wash them, and let it dry on their bodies. They were ready for next day and always clean.

Cucarachas and a new house

It was about the second night, when I woke up hearing a buzzing noise of fast wings. I could not imagine what it could be. I slept with a small flashlight under my head. Slowly I took it out and turned it on to see a horrific sight. It was a whole cloud of big *"cucarachas"* (roaches*)* flying and running in all directions across the room, seemingly not even noticing that I was under a sleeping bag.

It was as if I had a thick roach blanket over me. I could barely breathe I was afraid to make any noise. There were too many of them and my only resort was to retreat, inching very slowly further into the sleeping bag and covering my head as much as I could. I didn't see any movement or hear any sound from the family.

It seemed to me that the terrible noise lasted for hours. All I could think about was how many cucarachas had joined me in the sleeping bag.

I pretended to be a "stick," and breathed very slowly and prayed and prayed that God would take my fear away. I thought, "They are small animals. They will not harm me much." I knew God was with me. This was being a missionary. It was what I wanted and this was a part of it. I was totally unprepared for this. I tried to remember any word from the Bible that would help me. The one that came to mind was:

"They that hope in the Lord will renew their strength; they will soar as with eagles' wings. They will run and not grow weary walk and not grow faint.

Isa.40:31(TNAB)

I definitely needed my eagles' wings to get out of there (at least in my mind.) So I hoped in the Lord and finally morning came. It seemed as if nothing had happened. "It was a dream," I thought. Nevertheless, the regular eating time was shorter and the father spoke quickly, "We have to move out the house. The *cucarachas* have taken over the house I have sent word to the rest of the community and soon they will be coming to build another house a short distance away."

I rolled up my sleeping bag and was ready in no time to follow the others. We arrived where the men pointed out a place to rebuild not far from another neighbor. I looked back where we had lived the last couple of days. The house was on fire and suddenly it was gone. The father said something in *Quechua.* One of the older boys translated to me. He said, "The home was good to us for the time we were there."

People came from all directions. Men, women and the children seemed happy. Some women had bundles under their arms carrying whatever food they had to share during the day. It appeared to me the people had experienced this situation many times before. I could tell by the organized way everyone moved around each person knew what to do. I just tried to stay out of the way and be helpful where I could.

Young and old men were very busy clearing and preparing the squared place where the house was going to be. Others started bringing in the palm leaves, the bamboo for the floor, the walls and the corners. Some made the holes for the four corners.

After the materials were in, they put the logs in place and connected the square with plunks. When all this was secure, they started to work on the roof. It was quite a sight to see everyone working so diligently like busy bees.

The noise of the human voices, laughter, camaraderie, and children's play was going on when they had finished their job of carrying the bamboo. The bamboo sticks were taken to the older men to make the slashes which would allow the bamboo to be opened flat to get ready for the wall. The women were busily cooking for everyone. Occasionally one of them would carry the pot of f*ermented chicha* and a cup and offer a drink to each of the men working.

I decided that would be a good job for me, so I did it. I noticed that the more they drank the louder they talked while they were working.

Everyone was delighted to see the Sister working with him or her and offering *Chicha*. I could not understand what they said to each other or what they were laughing about but I felt very good to be useful. It took all that day and the next day to finish the house.

It was a very simple one-big-room house. That night, the house smelled so brand new and clean from the palm leaves and the bamboo that has its own unique fresh scent. The children were excited and happily jumping around. They enjoyed the new house with new corners to investigate.

When the children settled down, I started to sing with them again. I asked them to teach me one of their songs in Quechua. It was a lot of fun. They laughed a lot because I could not get it right away. Of course, they felt "smarter than the Sister." I felt I had been part of a very special event. They rapidly made a rectangular wood frame full of dirt for a cooking place - enough for two big pots in the middle of the house.

The chief came in to where I was and said to me, "Now that we have finished the house, tell us why you are here.

Many missionaries have come already. I want to hear from you." The commune planned to meet in the afternoon. Approximately sixty people were all huddled together in the new house. I started telling them my personal story about how I came to know Jesus. A young man translated for the older people.

"Would you like to hear about Jesus?" was my question. They were ready to listen. My complete personal testimony took quite a while, but we had time; no hurry, no agendas to follow, no telephone, no electricity, and no running water.

I told them as far as I can remember I had known Jesus. My family is Catholic; they were pioneers in the town, of Borja Quijos. Since the town was growing, a couple of families decided they needed a Priest to guide them and let them know about God. They went to ask the Cardinal in Quito for one. I was the first child born in that town.

I repeated the story I had told so many times to those who had ask. The missionaries I met in my early life made a big impression on me.

I wondered why they left their home, family, and country, to come and tell us about Jesus. They said because they believed God wanted them to tell the Good News of Jesus to people who had not heard. The missionaries provided a scholarship for me to attend a boarding school. I thought being a missionary Sister would be the best way to be close to God and do His will. Therefore, I went far away to a convent in the United States.

The Quechua people wanted to know about me as a person. "Why are you going out by yourself with no husband?" In their culture, women do not go by themselves. I unfolded my story; their acceptance was increasing and important for me.

I explained, "There will be a whole team coming that will be working with you on a regular basis. I am just visiting you to see how you are doing and what your needs are. They knew the Commune leaders were being trained and wanted to know how it is working in the different areas."

I stayed a couple more days there, spreading God's kingdom at every opportunity I had. We had another meeting specifically for sharing the Word of God. It was my time to tell many of the parables which they could relate to. I shared with them what Jesus had said in the sermon on the mountain. He tells who are the Blessed!

When I had to leave, another man from the commune accompanied me on the way back to the Mission Center. I felt richer than when I came. I had received more than what I gave. It was certainly a blessing for me to live there a short time and see with my own eyes how God was at work. These people were very close to God in their own way. Many times, I felt God telling me:

> *"Remove the sandals from your feet for the place where you stand is holy ground"*
>
> Ex. 3:5 (TNAB)

After that visit, my daily prayer of Mary became my own. Now it meant more and I proclaim it with all my heart.

> *My soul proclaims the greatness of the Lord, my spirit rejoices in God my savior. For he has looked upon his handmaid's lowliness behold, from now on will all ages call me blessed. The mighty One has done great things for me, and holy is his name. His mercy is from age to age to those who fear him. He has shown might with his arm, dispersed the arrogant of mind and heart.He has thrown down the rulers from their thrones but lifted up the lowly. The hungry he has filled with good things; the rich he has sent away empty. He has helped Israel his servant, remembering his mercy, according to his promise to our fathers, to Abraham and to his descendants forever."*
>
> Luke 1:46-55(TNAB)

It was easier the next time I went to another indigenous commune because I knew more of what to expect. Yet there were always new surprises and challenges I would have to face. Reverend Camarero used to say, "Maria Luisa, always be ready for emergencies and surprises. We live on emergencies most of the time." There was no time for boredom or getting on a routine. The hardest part of all was the feeling of loneliness, missing family and friends. In the vast wilderness, most of us had to be physically alone and only God would be our companion.

The eyes of a mouse

The Word of God was taking strong root. The Base Christian Communities had begun to work in some areas and that made it all worthwhile. Any sacrifice or difficulty was all in God's hands. God was in control, we just kept on.

During an overnight visit to a home, I heard a little sound like a very small animal running or eating. I turned on my trusty flashlight carefully, and cautiously flashed it on top of me. I saw a pair of bright eyes looking straight at me. It was a mouse! This time in one move, I kicked and squirmed until I was in the bottom of the sleeping bag, rolled in a fetal position, feeling safe. I needed to learn not to be so afraid. The indigenous people are one with nature. I wanted to be like that. I needed to listen to nature's way of communicating. I was learning while I observed. The little mouse was my teacher.

In another commune, the leaders were already running their community and played a big part in the celebration of the Mass. At the prayer for the faithful, the petitions and the music were all in their language. One woman who was in a leadership role had a beautiful soprano voice. When the time came for her to sing, she just soared. (Even now, I still feel goose bumps on my skin at the thought of her voice.) As she sang, she sounded like different kinds of birds. She truly praised and helped us all praise God. I have never heard before or since such an awesome voice. It was a heavenly experience to celebrate with them.

This same woman told me a miracle God granted her. It was amazing. She said, "The youngest of my children is a gift from God." She showed me who he was. One time when she was on her way home, she found a baby abandoned in the forest. It is the custom when twins are born for the weak child to be abandoned in a hammock by the road, hoping someone would find the baby and adopt him or her into their family.

"I heard a baby crying madly and it made me feel desperate. My youngest child was already four years old and I had no milk to feed this baby. I prayed to God, 'If you want me to take this baby, give me the milk.'

I sat down, held the crying baby to my old and shriveled breast and, the baby started to suck. To my surprise, the noises the baby was making caused me look down. I saw milk coming out. I knelt and thanked God. It was a miracle! When I arrived home, my husband was there and saw me coming with a baby in my arms, and the basket on my head."

He asked, "What is it?"

I told him, "A baby God gave to me." She explained her experience. Then she said, "From then on, the milk never stopped until the baby started eating food." The whole community knew about the miracle and because of that, everyone loved and respected the woman more. "Yes it was a miracle," I assured her. To my amazement, she repeated Mary's words, she had known by heart:

> "The Almighty has done great things for
> me, and holy is his name."

The healthy and happy child was about four years old when I met him. A missionary couple from Italy served the commune where this woman lived.

The lady missionary told the story that one day this woman who was to be her interpreter, was leading her to visit another community. She had said she did not speak Spanish but understood it very well. (She had the gift of tongues.)

They had to cross a river by walking through it. The missionary was crossing with no problem. The water was above her hip because she was tall and well built. She heard the woman leader speak in perfect Spanish saying, "Curse this race that made me so short," The water was getting up to her neck and what she was carrying on her back was already wet. When they finally crossed the river, they both laughed whole-heartedly, amazed of what came out of her mouth. "You said you don't speak Spanish," the missionary stated. Shyly she responded, "At times I do."

It was a different type of ministry for these wonderful people of God. I felt I would require more training; I needed to understand their culture and most of all to be able to speak their language.

This would take a long time. I will never forget all of their beautiful faces, smiles, shyness, and respect. It was a wonderful experience to live with them for a couple of days.

I left it in God's hands. Wherever He would send me, I would go, no matter what. I talked to God and Monsignor Gonzalo and left it at that. In the future assignments of communities and teams, my work with the Quechua community was not a part of my ministry.

Chapter 5

Monsignor the Good Shepherd

"I exhort you Shepherd the flock of God which is among you, serving as overseers, not by constraint but willingly not for dishonest gain but eagerly, not as being lords over those entrusted to you, but being examples to the flock."

1 Peter 5:1 (TNAB)

There was a sense of expectation in the air. Monsignor Gonzalo let us know that he would soon be coming to our home. Everyone was happy to hear the good news and looked forward to seeing him and talking to him. It was obvious the love and respect the missionaries had for him. He was a true shepherd.

We welcomed him at the airport. After he settled in his room, he came out to us. We gathered around to hear him. He appeared relaxed, joked a lot and told us he would be staying for a week. I was astounded that everyone called him; Gonzalo; it seemed to me a lack of respect.

There was no title before his name when addressing him not "Your Excellency" or "Bishop" or "Monsignor" or anything else. He was one of us and he wanted to be treated like that. He listened attentively to the missionaries as they shared what was going on in the Church.

Some plans had been presented concerning which communities needed a visit most from him. As a new person on the team, I was surprised to learn that he spends time and talks, not only with the heads of the different departments but also with everyone else, including the workers. He took time to know each one of us personally and to learn about our ministries.

He had a rich prayer life. After every meal, he would walk on the terrace praying, enjoying the sunrise or sunset over the Aguarico River. He prayed with the community of missionaries and led most of the prayers. He was regularly seen with his book of prayers at different times of the day. No matter where he was, he prayed. It was very inspiring to me.

When it was, my turn to talk to him, the first thing he said was "I have heard nothing but good reports about you. How you have integrated yourself into the team. You surprised everyone by how hard and how willingly you work. They did not expect that from someone coming from the USA"

I was surprised. It was a compliment and coming from him, it meant even more to me. I happily let him know how grateful and honored I was that he had accepted me. He had given me the opportunity to fulfill my dream of becoming a missionary. He had heard the story of my dream before and now he saw that it was becoming a reality.

Then he seriously said, "It is important to be educated in the ways and culture of the people you will be ministering to." He reminded me that Jesus became one of us and in the same way; we have to become one with the poor to whom we will be ministering. "The next thing I want you to do," he said, "is to be trained by spending time in another Diocese that has the same vision, experience how they minister to God's people, learn all you can and come back to us.

He continued, "I have been praying for your coming for fifteen years. You are exactly what I asked for." I was astounded. I could not believe my ears. I would have been content to hear him say I was doing a good job, but to hear him say, "I have been praying for your coming for fifteen years," made me speechless.

I prayed in my heart, "God if this is what you want, I am ready," I told Monsignor the same. He arranged for me to go to a seminar at Riobamba, the Capitol city of the Province of *Chimborazo* in *La Sierra.* Chimborazo is the highest Ecuadorian mountain and the third highest in America. This province has the largest concentration of indigenous people in Ecuador. Riobamba is the link between the coast and the highlands; one encounters indigenous people along with *mestizo* (a mix of Indian and white) and a minority of white people in the city.

Monsignor Proaño was the Bishop who headed the Center for Evangelization in Santa Cruz (a city in Los Andes) where he had started a new way of evangelizing. He has a great group from which we could learn much.

We would become part of a team which would participate in a week- long seminar to learn how to spread God's Kingdom in theory and in practice. When the time came to go there, I was ready. I love to travel. In this new experience, I would to learn how to understand the people better and delivered the Word of God to them.

Monsignor Gonzalo shared his own personal conversion in a Conference in Iquitos, how the Word became more alive to him while in a weeklong seminar in Peru. He wanted me to have that experience. I bless the Lord. I felt blessed myself, and all I could say, as Mary the mother of Jesus said when visited by the Angel Gabriel. "Be it done to me according to your word."

The Riobamba Educational Center for indigenous people, and those who wanted to work with them, was different from the one in Sucumbíos. The Center was already established. Although it was simple, it had better accommodations such as electricity and running water.

Santa Cruz in Riobamba was one of the first Dioceses in Ecuador that started working specifically with the indigenous people. Monsignor Proaño was lovingly called by everyone, "The Bishop of the Poor."

The agenda was clear. One day would be spent in the classroom learning in general how our relationship with God can be expressed in our relationship to the poor. Other themes were given to us to help the overall comprehension. I was hearing some quotes from the Bible for the first time. One example: *"To mock the poor is to insult his creator." (Prov.17:5).* This is at the very heart of Biblical faith. The prophet Amos is very fierce in this point when he says:

> *Listen to this word, you cows of Basham living in the mountains of Samaria, you who oppress the weak In addition, abuse the needy. Who say to your lords, Bring drink for us! The Lord God has sworn by his holiness: Truly, the days are coming upon you when they shall drag you away with hooks, the last of you with fishhooks; And you shall be cast into the mire, says the Lord.*
>
> *Amos 4:1-2 (TNAB)*

After listening to each lecture, we were given questions to discussion in small groups.

Then we would present our answers in a picture or in words for the whole group. Some questions pondered were as follows: "What does the subject, which was just presented say to you? Bring conclusions for your pastoral work. How do we recognize the suffering face of Jesus in the poor? How can we bring about a better world for all? What is the distinction between faith and ideology? Remember, bringing the good News of Jesus is Evangelization."

The next day we visited various communities in teams of two and came back at the end of the day to report on what we accomplished. The third day we returned to the classroom. We evaluated our visits, read the Word of God, meditated, and received more input from the seminar leader. We began to comprehend what needed to be done. Then we came up with a resolution and finally we celebrated.

At this point, the picture began to unfold even more and my eyes were open to understanding what the Vicar Reverend Camarero had explained to me on orientation day.

I realized it would take much time, learning through actual practice on the mission field before it could truly become a part of me. However, I was ready.

My heartfelt refreshed like the onset of springtime, though I did not exactly know what had come over me. Everyone noticed the expression on my face and remarked about it in their small groups. I felt elated. It was as if I were being fed a new kind of food and new wine physically, emotionally and spiritually. One of the leaders said to me, "You have no idea what I thought about your coming from the States. I was reluctant to let you join us because I thought you would have a poor attitude. I wondered if you would be able to work with the poor." I was learning how to spread the Word of God in this new way, which was to listen first and get them ready to hear the Word of God. This way made more sense than the traditional way I knew.

We had one more day to visit and do pastoral work in the field. The last day of the seminar would be for more evaluation. My mind and way of viewing God through these talks and experiences had been stretched and challenged to new horizons.

My previous views changed little by little, and my spirit was soaring. It also helped that this area was so different geographically from the one in the jungle, where I was ministering before.

Riobamba is part of La Sierra region, which is a very cold with high bare mountains. You can only see hay fields incessantly being blown by a cold wind in a wave-like motion. It had its own beauty that could be appreciated as God's creation, once you bundled up comfortably. The children with their red cheeks, dry, cracked, scaly skin, running noses, ragged clothes and no shoes, told the obvious story of how poor the people in this area were. It was a painful sight, yet their faces radiated joy.

There was no electricity, no running water. The people made their own houses of adobe. Everyone, men, women and children alike wore a *poncho or zarape* and a hat or a cape. As we walked or drove down the road, we could see young children taking care of sheep.

Their living accommodations were usually a one-room hut with a fireplace in the middle used for cooking and warming the house. The beds were against the adobe walls. Everything took place in this one room and around the fire. Those who were economically better off had more rooms but their homes were still made of adobe.

In the evening, family and friends sat around the fire to tell stories and share what had happened during the day. They lived in poverty yet the people appeared to be happy, satisfied, peaceful, and grateful for all they did have.

It was such a contrast to living in the States. There comfort and material possessions are important and community living is foreign to their culture. Yet here it was very clear for anyone to see; these people were very rich in spirit, and contented in the simplicity of life. They cared for one another. Jesus' words came to mind

"Happy are the poor in spirit for theirs is the kingdom of heaven.

Matt 5:3

This was another very enriching experience. At the completion of the seminar I returned to La Mission Carmelita to practice what I had learned and experienced by observing the way the missionaries' modeled Christian living.

After a year had passed, Monsignor Gonzalo informed us he wanted some of us missionaries to attend a course on Liberation Theology in Lima, Peru given by the theologian Gustavo Gutierrez. I was delighted to be part of the team assigned to go and learn what this much-respected author had to say.

Lima Peru, Liberation theology

I had heard the theology before; I was trying to put it into practice. I knew who Gustavo Gutierrez was.

I thought I would finally be enlightened. I wanted to hear Gustavo Gutierrez explain what the Theology of Liberation really is.

What I heard was good, and now I better understood. I heard about Gustavo Gutierrez's life.

He told of his personal conversion while reading the Word of God. It was inspiring to hear how he started spreading this inspiring new way of looking at God. It was from the biblical viewpoint of the poor. Those who were exploited and despised but were very much loved by God and His Son Jesus Christ.

It started to make more sense as he read the following paragraph from the Bible. Gustavo read very emphatically. I could easily imagine Jesus saying this with such inner power and authority.

> *"The spirit of the Lord God is upon me,*
> *because the Lord has anointed me.*
> *He has sent me to bring good news to the poor.*
> *To heal the broken hearted....*

Isa.61:1-2 (TNAB)

We needed to reflect, as God told the prophet, to eat the scroll, to chew it. The need for a new approach to Christian spirituality in Latin America was apparent now. The need to take care of the whole person, not just the "soul" was evident. We needed to see that the life of the Church is not only a theological place but is doing theology in practice.

Lima, Peru was an unexpected sight for me. It is an old Colonial City with beautiful Spanish architecture. The traces of smog everywhere made an impression on me. The dark ashes on top of the white paint gave a dismal colorless picture. The city was built in a desert but a river runs through the city. It does not rain as it does in Ecuador. There was not a good water drainage system and the odor was strong. There were not many facilities, such as public restrooms. Poverty was all around.

In some areas, the walls and roofs of the houses are made of straw mats. Two times, it drizzled while we were there and the people panicked. Some locals commented saying, "We are not used to rain. It never rains in Lima." The dryness was suffocating for me, and every afternoon I would hope and pray it would rain to clear the air and clean the streets. A real rain never came.

We attended classes at the University of, Lima Peru and stayed at *"El barrio Miraflores."* I discovered later on this was one of the better neighborhoods of Lima. The Dominican

Sisters live there and gave us a place to stay. We walked a couple of blocks every day to catch a bus that took us to the university.

There was silence in the streets - no music from any of the houses. It was unusual for me not to hear it after living in East Los Angeles, California USA and Quito, Ecuador. There music from cars, radios and people playing tape recorders is blasting for the entire neighborhood to hear.

One afternoon we finished early and went to visit a downtown church. It is typical in some cities in South America to have small businesses located in front of the church for tourist and locals to buy small trinkets, candles, key chains, fruit, candy, etc.

We saw and heard a woman screaming at a four year old child. She had a whip in her hand and said, "I told you to stay put and take care of the table. The thieves are ready to steal." (The mother had been talking to her neighbor and had left the responsibility to the child.)

I have no idea what came over me but as I got close to her, the child looked at me with eyes pleading for help. He was about to be badly beaten and I could not stand to watch injustice being done to this weak, helpless child. I surprised myself at my quick reaction.

I took the whip from the woman's hand, and said: "Please, do not hit the child!" She was astonished that a stranger would do that. The child saw me react. He ran quickly for safety and disappeared.

I also ran, threw away the whip, joined the Sisters and mingled in the crowd. I was afraid she might want to whip me now. I prayed that the woman would not recognize me when we came out of the Church. Inside the Church, I prayed for that child and his mother. I had no idea of the full situation. However, God knew and only He could intervene. I guess all the talks about defending the poor had energized me to act.

The Theologian Gustavo Gutierrez was a short, vibrant Priest, with a lot of conviction as he talked. At one point during a passionate delivery of the message, he climbed up on top of the desk so we could all see him. I was overjoyed to hear him. He shared his very humble background; how he was the only one in his family who had the opportunity to study and how he had encountered God in a new way by reading the Bible from the perspective of the poor.

At the lecture, there were people of all backgrounds, social classes, and nationalities.

During the conference, the leaders suggested we meet some new people every day. Our discussions were done by two's or three's during the conference. I encountered a young woman from Brazil who spoke Portuguese but understood Spanish I understood Portuguese. We were able to communicate very well. She had a good understanding of the concepts of the Spirituality of Liberation Theology. We received a very simple outline worksheet of the conference for every topic.

At the next discussion time, I met another interesting person, an older indigenous woman. She was intensely paying attention and reacting in the right moments, or making comments about the talk. She was the leader of a community from the high mountains of Peru. She had walked all day before catching a bus so she could learn from Gustavo. I wished I had more time to talk with her and listen to her wisdom and sound thinking.

She spoke of how her community was asleep but now is growing in wisdom and understanding of the Word of God.

She said, *"Our eyes are open now."* My own prejudiced way of thinking and the walls I had built against the uneducated over the years were now challenged. I never saw her again; she has made a difference in my way of thinking. New horizons were now part of my view of life. Those walls were beginning to crumble down as in *Jericho*.

The organizer gave us instructions as to where we could find more literature about the subjects that interested us. One afternoon some of us decided to take a bus to go to town on a shopping adventure. The Sisters had warned us, "Take only the money you intend to spend, no more. Take good care of your purse and watch out for anyone around you."

Each one of us was alert, yet on the bus it was difficult to watch who came close. All of us were squeezed together like sardines on the bus. I wanted to make sure my money was safe. It was in my small agenda where I kept my addresses and emergency telephone numbers.

The strap on my shoulder let me hold my bag in front of me. I covered it with both hands. I was right behind the driver looking through the mirror.

On my way out of the bus when it was time to pay the fare, I put my hand in my bag and found absolutely nothing. My handbag had a cut about three inches long on the side and left me penniless. I showed the driver. With an understanding look, he only made a sign for me to get off the bus. I was in shock; trembling but grateful I was not hurt. Now I could not even buy a post card. My friends paid for the fare back when we finished shopping.

It was time to visit some communities. We went by two's to visit the city slums *(Pueblos Jóvenes)!* I was very interested in the children happily playing at the water fountain. One of the locals said, "That is how the children take a shower." At the same time, children and women were getting water in their buckets to carry home. All around Lima, there were slums showing deep poverty where much work needed to be done.

Some places had started to build a *"Base Christian Community."* Some were not organized yet, and some had just started to hear the *Word of a God* "who listens to the voice of the poor and cares for them."

To understand the new concepts, we had to go back to the Sacred Scripture "The Bible", and to the Documents of Vatican II, Medellin y Puebla. He talks of the new structures of the church.

Reverend Gutierrez had developed a spirituality which grew out of his life experience and ministering to Latin American people. Rooted in the reality of oppression and repression of the poor, he called for conversion from self-complacency and self-sufficiency to solidarity with the poor. Through the practice of the people, they themselves have learned and discovered this new way of reading God's Word.

Reverend Gutierrez quoted Vallejo a couple of times. Vallejo, like Job, brought a suit against God because of the suffering he endured. How many of us have an experience like it?

However, he too was able to meet God and enjoy His presence with tenderness and confident understanding. This had such a resounding tone for me that I read it many times.

My cup overflowed, I needed to be able to pass on what I had learned. Abundant blessings had come to me. I was determined to share them with others and multiply those blessings as the seed that was planted in good ground to give forth a hundred fold.

In the short time I stayed at the Sucumbíos Church, I perceived how much the people were ready and thirsty to hear and put into practice the Word of God. With every breath I took, I experienced God's love and His challenge to me. All I could say was, "Thy will be done in me."

After this course, more important responsibilities were given to me. At the next Assembly of missionaries, Bishop Gonzalo arranged for me to head the Department for Women's Development and Evangelization. This meant I had to travel all over the Mission area to see how each center was doing.

Chapter 6

The Life Cycle From Birth To Death

"The one who sent me is with me. He has not left me alone, because I always do what is pleasing to Him."

John 8:29 (TNAB)

Via Quito Km.5 was a very small community. The missionaries had been ministering there for awhile. The people were organized enough to have their own leaders who knew the process of building a "Basic Christian Community." The people were very friendly. When the missionaries let it be known they were coming for a regular visit, the leaders would send word to each member and gather at the school for the reunion.

The people lived close to the school where the meetings were held. The children had Religion and Bible classes taught by the missionaries after regular school hours. They loved to sing and I loved to play the guitar for them. At times we danced, just enjoying ourselves while learning about Jesus. "Let the children come to me."

I wanted so much for those children to know Jesus as their friend, Savior and Lord and for them to find all the answers for a better life in Him and with Him. Though it was very difficult at times to carry the guitar, it was useful, and the joy it brought to the children made it worthwhile.

In the evening at the community meeting the family was together. The agenda was to first follow up on what had happened after the last visit. How were they managing? What are the new needs? Have they been meeting weekly? The leader and the other members responded. This evaluation would help us to see if they were growing spiritually and what their needs were. (See picture #5)

After the meeting we gathered together to worship. At the celebration of Mass, the people would pray for their personal needs and those of the community. It was amazing to see the Holy Spirit at work.

The prayers usually were according to their needs; someone sick, someone died, someone was in jail, another needs help with their sick animals, or cutting down trees to be able to plant bananas, corn, or coffee. Then it was time to give thanks and celebrate.

On one of the visits I had with them, an unexpected request came to me. It happened while I was teaching the children about our faith. The after school-program was just before the adult meeting and Mass. (see picture #6)

Nancy a teenager came from another community much farther away in the jungle. She came to let us know that her uncle George had died. She asked if the Priest would be able to go and celebrate Mass at her home. I said, "Yes. He will come later and I will let him know." I was sure he would say, "Yes." She went ahead to prepare for the visit.

When the Priest came, I informed him of the request. He did not say much in response, and went on with what is usually done in a community visit. Later on he told me he was surprised I had said "Yes"

We held the meetings, and he let the people know of the death in the neighboring community some distance from where we were. We celebrated Mass and some people decided to accompany the missionaries to be with the family in this time of sorrow.

Time went by quickly and soon it was dark. At the same time I observed that the men were preparing torches, (long sticks with some old rags tied to it) that they dipped into diesel fuel to light. I was dressed in blue jeans, a very light white blouse and tennis shoes. I did not realize the evening would be chilly. I was not ready in any way; except I had the desire to help. The torches were lit and we slowly started the unexpected and very eventful journey.

As we started walking, the loud varied noises of the night animals frightened me terribly. I felt comfortable to ask a little girl if we could go together. Alma was her name, about 9 years old.

She smiled happily; proud I had chosen her as my companion while giving me her hand. I held her hand as if my life depended on it.

I felt that being a missionary, I must be the strong one and not be afraid, but for some reason I could not help it, I was frightened. It was so dreadfully dark; I could not see where to put my foot for the next step. I had to trust the little girl and let her lead me, I felt literally blind. I was walking in faith.

Silently, I was praying and asking God to protect me and help me in this frightful time. The different Psalms I knew, I repeated in my mind to keep calm, asking for Gods protection. "The Lord is my shepherd there is nothing I shall want," I said over and over. I sang songs like. "Do not be afraid." I sang and prayed whatever I could think of to help my quivering heart calm down and be at peace as I followed the lead of my faithful companion.

The tennis shoes were not much protection for my legs in the muddy road. It was a horse's trail, so there were lots of deep holes with a long horse step in between. Alma, who was very light on her feet, almost flew over the mud. I invariably got stuck and slowed her down. I could see the torches way ahead or behind us but not right where we were.

There were about twenty people going to accompany the family. In the movies, I had seen people walking in the dark with torches. It seemed so easy then but now for me it was real and very difficult. It would have been impossible to see the way without the torches.

I have no idea how long we had been walking when above the noises of the night animals I heard some far away sound of running water. It became louder and closer. The line of people, one at a time stopped ahead, talked, and kept going. When I made it to the place where people were stopping, my heart felt like it was going to burst out of fear.

Alma let go of my hand and went ahead. Way down, I could hear the deep noise of the waterfall. It was so dark I could see nothing. The ladies, children, young and old men kept passing by me. I realized I was paralyzed with fear. My feet would not obey me. In front of me there was a thin log used as a bridge. Above me there was a bamboo pole to hold on to.

Finally one of the men came to me and sounding concerned said, "You are the last one.

If you don't want to stay here and spend the night alone, you have to cross here. Sister, with your left hand hold on to my back pack and I will go slowly. Put your feet sideways on the thin log and hold on to the bamboo with your right hand. The log may be slippery."

I told him, "I want to go but my legs won't obey me. I don't know what to do." He explained at length the dangers of the night if I chose to stay there. I would have to stay by myself. Well, the reality just described by this man was worse than crossing the bridge. One inch at a time I crossed the river. When I got to the other side, the Priest's face was white as a sheet looking at me.

I wondered how I looked. I ran and hugged him and cried. He apologized for letting me go and not explaining what it meant to go to that community. He saw the terror in my face and my tears. I was glad most of the people were ahead and did not see the release of my expression of fear.

(I must tell you, many years after this experience, I found out the root of my fear of crossing any body of water during the day or night.

While I, was studying to be a hypnotherapist. I was hypnotized.) I was able to remember details of an early childhood trauma of crossing a river. During the session I saw I was about four years old. My oldest brother Aurelio asked me if I wanted to go to the river with him. Of course I said, "Yes" and happily followed him. He was carrying a solid iron wheel to hook over a cable that went across the river.

After some walking, he carried me on his shoulders the rest of the way. He said he was going to visit his girl friend. We climbed the bamboo ladder to the platform where he hung the iron wheel on the cable, to cross the river. This was the only way to get across. Then he tied himself with a rope making a seat, and sat me on his knees, securing me with a rope to his body. We crossed the river. I felt happy and safe with my brother.

When we arrived at the other side of the river, he said, "This is as far as you come with me. Now you go back. Other people will need the wheel to cross the river. It has to be at the house." I was shocked when he said that. I started weeping.

"I cannot do that, I am afraid." He said, "Just don't look down at the water," he tied me into the rope seat and with a big push, he sent me off to the middle of the river. I had no idea how long I was there nor how I managed to get to the other side. My next memory was feeling the warm sand on my bare feet after I went down the ladder, hanging the heavy wheel on my shoulder. That experience had marked me for life. So walking in the dark in the jungle and crossing a thin log called a bridge was one more traumatic horror for me.

When we arrived at the house, people were already there with the niece who was the only relative in this area. After introductions and small talk, we gathered to pray. We were all standing around the table where the deceased person lay, covered with a white sheet. There were candles around his body and some jungle flowers. It is customary to celebrate the Eucharist, (Mass). One of the readings was from the book of Ecclesiastes 3: 1 "This was a time to mourn."

Usually family, relatives and friends spend the night with the dead, praying, singing, and talking.

The niece told us her uncle caught a cold, and got worse and died. He did not think it was serious enough and the great distance to the doctor prevented him from making the trip. Later, as he became more seriously ill, he was not able to travel. She said, "We had no money for the doctor." We all understood that.

After Mass, we had something to eat. We took turns during the night leading the Rosary, prayers, Psalms, singing, reflecting on God's Word. This was a time to consider the shortness of life. Any one of the leaders besides the Priest could help in the reflection. Death can come any time. We need to be prepared to make the most of our lives.

In the small house, there was no place to sit. We had to spend the night mostly standing up. Some men were talking outside. Most of the women were in the kitchen. If there was silence, it was because we were falling asleep standing up. We could not move because we were packed in like sardines.

The men drank cinnamon tea with hard liquor to keep warm and stay awake. The women drank tea without the liquor.

It is customary at this time to tell stories of the life of the deceased person; some sad, some funny and some serious. When the stories of his suffering came out, many people cried for him with the niece. Some said, "He is not suffering any more. He is with God." The young Spanish Priest was silent most of the time after the celebration of the Mass. I believe it was his first experience of a death in the new world.

The women talked about the terrible situation that awaited the niece. Now she would be by herself. Some leaders said, "We the community have to do something, because of this great need. It is a challenge God has sent our way." With the leadership of the Priest, we prayed and discerned how to help her in practical ways.

It was clear she could not stay by herself in that house alone in the middle of nowhere. There were dangers that could come from nature, animals, or other human beings.

Some women volunteered to let her stay in their home while she was figuring out what to do.

It would take a long time to get the news to the rest of the family back in Loja. It was on the other side of the country. We needed to find out when or if someone would be coming to be with her.

She chose the neighbor closest to her home which allowed her to continue taking care of the home and the animals. They had a couple of pigs, chickens, and a dog that needed daily care.

About 4:00 a.m. as dawn started to break, the roosters crowed and the men began to look for wood to make a coffin. The women and children went to catch some chickens, peeled yucca and bananas, and cooked breakfast for all the people that had spent the night in the house. Each one of us had something to do. We took turns bringing in wood for the fire, peeling yucca, green bananas and minding the pots. Some people stayed with the cadaver (corpse) praying in silence.

As the sun peeked out giving its light through the forest, we started eating. We ate in small groups, the number being determined by how many dishes the family had and what other families brought with them for the occasion.

The men were just about ready with the coffin. After breakfast it was finished. We prayed again and the men reverently put the dead man's body into the coffin and closed it.

I did not ask if we were going back the same way we came. I was terribly embarrassed about my fear of crossing the river. However, now that it was light, I thought it might be different. In the meeting, I overheard the men saying, "We have a long way to go and it will take much time to go back because we have to carry the coffin."

The burial in the catholic cemetery was important. The uncle could not be buried anywhere else. It was normal for them to find a way to the cemetery and now the challenge was to cross the river. Some of the men knew of a place where the river was not so deep and people could cross easier.

"We need a horse for the women and children to cross the river," one of the men said. Jorge, a young man, volunteered to go to the next community to borrow a horse from someone he knew.

I felt relieved, knowing I would not have to go back the same way we came. The way back was longer, but in the daylight, I could see where we were going. The trail was less traveled and it was less of a hardship for me. The procession started very slowly. When the river showed its banks, it was smooth and wide.

The men started crossing. Four men at a time took turns carrying the coffin. The long procession was broken by the children and women who had to cross by horseback. Jorge took women and children on the horse, one or two at a time. We had to put our feet as high as we could so as not to get wet and catch a cold later on. Some of us got wet anyway because occasionally the horse missed a step and almost lost his passenger.

Jorge would cross the river, let us get off the horse, and turn around and go back to bring the next one in line. This activity took a long time and gave the men who carried the coffin time to get ahead of us.

The terrain was very challenging not to drop the coffin for those men carrying it.

There was no road, and the trail was narrow, full of trees, bushes, roots and holes to get around or through. They walked very slowly. I do not know how they did it but they did!

This was a time to realize life is short and we will all die someday. Are we ready to meet the Lord? We must believe that His son Jesus died to pay the penalty for our sins and forgives us, so that we can stand perfect before God through Christ's perfection. The mood was sober. Finally in the middle of the afternoon, we arrived at the cemetery where the burial ground was ready.

The rest of the community, who did not go to the house and spend the night, was waiting for us to arrive with the coffin. They joined the procession and went to the cemetery to bury him. As usual, the Priest blessed the grave, prayed, and then we sang. The leaders of the community and other people joined in and prayed for the deceased man's meeting God; that he would rest in peace with Jesus. We sang for a long time and also cried together.

The leaders invited all of us to go to the school (used for community meetings) for the meal where there was plenty food for all. It reminded me of the "Multiplication of the loaves and fishes." I felt so grateful to God and amazed at how these Christians act who really know God. These people, as poor as they were, brought what they had to share with everyone in our time of need.

What a lesson. The word of God was falling on good ground, and was giving much fruit and fruit that will last. I humbly accepted that God had chosen me to be a part of this experience. I thought I was bringing the good news of Jesus to them, and also, they brought Jesus to me in a very practical and obvious way.

Every time I went to visit that community, Alma always came to hug me. She was the one who had led me in the dark and stayed by my side as my guardian angel. I was so proud of her. During the class, I took time to explain how brave Alma had been and how she helped me. It was a way to make them aware that adults are also fearful of the unknown. They applauded her. She was being recognized for that deed.

I loved her and could not have done without her help that night. I felt very humbled how a child's strength had given me power and we became closer for it. It was a mutual admiration. From that time on and many times afterwards, I would feel her adoring brown eyes on me.

In another one of my regular weekly visits to this community, a little girl name Mercedes invited me to visit her mother who had just had a baby girl. I promised I would go the next week. This time I was ready. I wore boots and suitable clothes for the occasion, just in case I needed them. Mercedes told me it was not far. Right after classes, we started walking. The trail was clear and she was skipping over the bumps on the way, as happy as could be. I was just delighted to see her happiness and joy. But I was getting weary and kept asking how much farther we needed to go. Each time she answered with a big bright smile, "Just a little more."

As the sun began to set, the monkeys came out swinging from tree to tree, almost like an honor guard in a double line at each side of the trail.

Their loud communication started to frighten me. Mercedes seemed to be familiar with them, as if they were her long-time friends. They were adding to their number as we went, making louder and louder noises. Once more I thought I needed to trust God, that he wouldn't abandon me. It helped to see the child did not look or act afraid.

I wished so much I could enjoy and understand what the monkeys were doing or saying but I knew no monkey language. They watched us, so I suggested to Mercedes, "We may as well start singing and see what will happen." So we did. The monkeys stopped as if to listen. I found my answer so we sang loudly all the rest of the way home. When we finally arrived, I asked Mercedes where the bathroom was before going into the house. I needed to go desperately. She pointed in a direction. I was expecting to see a small shed of some kind but I could not see it anywhere. She told me, "It is there, I will show you."

She took me by the hand behind a coffee bush. Sure enough, there was a small hole and residues of the last occupant remained.

I asked her to move away a bit and watch for any newcomers, so she did. The dogs were the first ones to know we were there but they were friendly and played with her.

The homes are usually built about six feet off the ground for safety's sake, because of the night animals. There was a strong ladder which I climbed in order to meet her mother and the other children three- year-old Jose, five-year-old Gladys and the baby. Doña was smiling and said, "I am so glad you made it, Sister. I was afraid we would have to eat our chicken by ourselves." She had made a special dinner. She was so hospitable and her house was so shining clean you could have eaten off the floor. I wondered about how much time this lady must have spent cleaning the *"chonta floor."* (Chonta is a kind of palm, very strong) It shined brightly. It was unusual to have this type of floor because normally it would have been made of bamboo. This floor was elegant, expensive and harder to work with.

She said her husband would be coming home soon from work with her older son.

We talked about how she had given birth alone. She said, "God and Mother Mary were with me, and a neighbor came to help me." The baby was healthy and asleep at the time. After dinner, when the baby awoke I held her, another beautiful brown-eyed girl. When the father and teenage son came home, they washed their hands and soon we were eating soup and chicken, fried bananas and rice.

When I commented to Pedro how hard he must have worked to build the house and have that type of floor, he replied, "God has been good to us. There is so much chonta on my land, which is native to this area. The neighbors came to help build the home before the baby came."

Mercedes was so very proud to have brought me to her home. Now I had another very special friend. I would have missed so much if I had not gone on this visit. They expressed how much my visit meant to them.

I thanked God for giving me the desire and the energy to do what I thought was definitely His will. As it started to get dark, Pedro sent his son Luis, a thirteen-year- old young man, to fetch the horses.

He said, "Luis will take you to the road to catch a ride. The buses go by regularly at this time." I was delighted to have a companion and a horse to ride. It was only a twenty minute horseback ride but for me it seemed an eternity because of the darkness.

Luis came in and said, "The horses are ready." I said the usual goodbyes, kissed the baby and promised to visit again. Catalina said, "Soon I hope to be at the community meeting."

It is customary for some women (depending on the region they come from.) who had just had a baby to stay in the house for 40 days. After forty days the mother goes to offer the child to God during Mass. It is a very important and meaningful ceremony. When I came out of the house, getting down the ladder was easier than going up. Luis had said the horses were ready but the horses I saw had no saddle.

"Well another experience," I told to myself. I told Luis, "Go slowly because I am not sure of my horse-riding skills without a saddle." He laughed and told me. "It is very easy. The horses know the way. Just relax and let them walk."

Then he proceeded to show me by jumping on one. I had to be helped by Pedro to get on the horse. He reassured me that I would not have a problem with this horse. He was a very gentle horse which had been trained to be ridden by women.

I started to ride. I prayed and talked to the horse all the way. I knew from experience a horse's ears tell a story. The horse's ears will stand up straight when there is danger or something unusual. I kept my eyes on the horse's ears and let the horse lead me.

We arrived at the school. The road ran right in front of the school. This is where the bus stopped. I picked up my guitar and waited a short time. The bus picked me up. When Luis saw me in the bus, he waved goodbye and went back home.

I had time to meditate and pray, thanking God for these people and this memorable experience. Their goodness and generosity for me were a reflection of God's greatness. I kept experiencing that God never leaves me alone. He has always been with me. As I do His will and spread the Word and His kingdom in this part of the world.

My heart at times felt like bursting for sheer joy. God was at work in all the people I met and came in contact with.

I prepared many of the children here to receive Jesus. It was such a joy to get them ready for the day. Their innocence and transparent souls encouraged me many times. I felt very much loved by them and whatever they could bring as a gift, they did. Sometimes a beautiful jungle flower, a twig, or anything they found interesting on the way to school. I looked forward to visiting this community and working with the children and women.

Chapter 7

Living in Christian Unity

"He said to them in reply, "My mother and my brothers are those who hear the Word of God and act on it."

Luke 8: 21 (TNAB)

Since my arrival on November 14, 1998, the Aguarico Carmelite Mission Center became my home. From here, I would go to the different communities with various missionaries in order to get acquainted with the pastoral work, the people, and note how evangelization was being done in this Church.

Aguarico Community became one part of my ministry while living there. It was located by the shore of the Aguarico River just across from the mission center. From the top of the hill across the river, we could see the ladies washing their clothes, draping on top of the rocks and bushes for them to dry.

It was a very rewarding experience to minister to the people and to watch them grow and work together for the betterment of the whole community. We had to cross the river many times to visit different communities in the area.

We used the ferry that carried mainly Texaco company cars and equipment. The people would just jump on the platform of the ferry and cross with the vehicles. At times the river rose and the current was very strong because of the constant rain. You could see trees and all kinds of rubbish, even big snakes in the water. Then only a few canoes and daring experts were able to cross the river.

Once when the river had risen through the night I was shocked by the high water. It was flowing very rapidly. Reverend Landeira and I had been scheduled for a community visit. I saw how frightening this enormous body of water was and I asked, "Do you think we should go back? We can't cross it like this and I am really afraid." I had my guitar in one hand and a small overnight bag in the other. In response to my fearful concern, he replied, "I am also trembling," and with that comment he proceeded to continue to get into the canoe. I silently followed, praying that this would not be my time to meet God.

Highlights of Aguarico

I will focus on four of the highlights of my ministry at Aguarico Community, although there were many others. We had a good program going for the whole family, including working with the children after school. It was important to introduce them to Jesus as a person, the Son of God who gave His life for us and we did this through lessons, songs, games, plays, etc.

Once a week in the late afternoon, we had a very active youth group. The Pope in his apostolic exhortation says.[2] "The Church pays special attention to young people." Then he emphasized the need for young people who were well informed about their faith and well rooted in prayer to become apostles among other young people. "The church was called to carry the gospel to the ends of the world. Young apostles need a profound spirituality that gives them strength and courage for their apostolic work in a difficult environment and with young people who are passing through critical life situations." This philosophy could be found in the Base Christian Community.

We had a program for the women once a week that included Bible reading, examining the Biblical texts about women and Jesus, reading from the woman's point of view, understanding the personal struggles and needs of each woman, and finally the freedom that Jesus brings to us. As a result of all of our studying, and understanding of the Word of God, we brought about much needed solidarity and unity among women. We also had parenting, sewing, general hygiene, health and cooking classes as well as classes on how to take care of their finances.

Once a week in the evening we had classes for everyone who wanted to learn how to read and write. It was very important to develop trust among them in the light of the Word of God. The ladies in the group would be searching for personal transformation, understanding of the church and society.

Besides our weekly program, the Priest came to celebrate Mass once a month. We were working together to better the community as a whole.

The mission center was close to this community, whenever there was a need, someone would come to request our presence in addition to the visits made to the community on a regular basis.

Free the captives

One such time came when one of the ladies told us at the meeting that her husband had been taken to jail. He had been wrongly accused by a wealthy person who had both the judge and the police on his side. We prayed and read the Word of God seeking direction as to what we would do. After much deliberation, we decided it would be best to go directly to the jail, talk to the sheriff, and the police and any other authority there. If they would not listen we would go to the governor.

When we arrived at the jail it was a great encouragement and strength to have a large number of supporters with us. Whenever something like this happened it was not unusual for people to gather, so we had some curious individuals added to our number. The sheriff listened as we presented our case.

Ahead of time, we planned who would speak and when one of us stopped or could not find words to express our situation. Another would take over the explanation. We were careful not to talk all at once and did a great job with good arguments and eye witnesses to the injustice being done to this poor man.

After a long time of listening to us he read the report one more time, and to our surprise he agreed with us. He apologized that his office did not do a good job in their investigation before putting the man in jail. He let the man go free and we took him home. We thanked God for His intervention. Justice had been done. At the next meeting, we again celebrated, giving thanks to God for the wonderful works he has done in and through us.

The power of Godly women

The next situation required much more effort and organization because of the serious circumstances. The city was going to build a road. It would be advantageous to a certain man if it passed around his land because his land would certainly go up in price. There was already a public trail across his property.

It was a shorter route and made it easier for the children to walk to school, especially when it rained and flooded. The land owner had already talked to the contractor to be sure the road went around his property to only his advantage.

A community meeting was called. The school teacher was present who was in accord with us and willing to support us. He understood the benefit for the students and the entire community. We decided to stop the road graders and huge bulldozers to prevent the opening of another road. The danger for the children would increase if the new road was further away from civilization. When the rains came, there would be flooding. I had seen children in other areas walk, with the water up to their necks. Then they would become sick with respiratory illness, not to mention the dangers of drowning. We did not want this to happen here.

Early the next day, two of us missionaries were there, with God's help, to put an end to this situation. We had seen the heavy equipment on the ferry that crossed the river. We knew they were arriving to start opening the road. (See picture #7)

We ran ahead and sent word to all of the mothers and children to come to the location where the machinery was already working. All the men of the community were at work. The women came from all around. Word of mouth had even brought some of those who were not present at the meeting.

As we saw the bulldozers coming in, we made a human wall at the place where we did not want the road to go through. We were either holding hands or were arm in arm. The pregnant ladies and the ones with infants were in the front line. Behind them were the older ladies with grandmas standing as a great wall. After them was another line of young teenage girls.

As a goodwill gesture, we had lemonade prepared for the workers but to our dismay, a new development came. One of the ladies said, "Last night the teacher was taken to a club by the land owner who proceeded to get him drunk." We were counting on his support but, he was sick, and had changed his mind. He would not come and be part of this demonstration. After talking it over, we decided to stick with our plan and let nothing stop us. We were certain that God was on our side. We started praying the Rosary and singing out loud. As the machinery came closer to us, we were becoming very apprehensive and we sang louder.

We remembered Gods words in *Isaiah: "Do not be afraid I am with you."* We realized the scriptures were our key to victory.

We had faith that the men driving these machines would stop their forward progress and would not hurt us. Some of their own families were in the line. Yet we could not be too sure because this was their work and livelihood. The men had received the order about where the road was to be built and were told not to stop for anything.

As they got closer and closer the noise of the machines and the trees falling was deafening. We had promised one another to stand together and not run. The mothers had a hard time holding on to their small children so that they would not run.

The closer they came the louder we sang. At times we even screamed.

Fear would not stop us. We needed to stand for what was best for the community and show that our strength was in God, for He is love and Justice.

After some frightening moments, the drivers of the equipment stopped and made the turn to where the old trail had been in use before. We cheered, we praised God aloud, and we embraced one another. The young ladies then went to offer lemonade to the men driving the machines. This was all part of the plan.

We continued praying as the work progressed. The owner sent a message that this road would go across his land "over his death body" and that he would "lie down across the old road so that the machines would not go there." However, the road went exactly in the location we had asked the city to build it. This was accomplished through God's power as a result of our petition to Him.

The plan was if the man did lie in the road, we (the younger stronger women) would pick him up and drop him to the side! He never showed up! We had a big laugh imagining four of us picking up that skinny short man and tossing him out of the way.

It was such a success that everyone was overwhelmed by what we could do with God on our side and working together. We won this time. This success was proof that, *"The Lord hears the cries of the poor."* We just needed to cooperate with one another. The next community meeting was held as a celebration of thanksgiving for what God had done for His people.

This success strengthen us

After one of the night classes for the community, there was a misunderstanding. It was the case of a jealous husband. During the class, a young man went to ask a question from one of the ladies about how to do the exercise. The husband had observed this and waited until he and his wife arrived home, at which time he became violent. He accused her of flirting and being unfaithful to him.

He did not attend the Christian Community meetings, but only went to the classes to learn how to read and write. He continued to ask why the man asked his wife instead of the teacher or another older woman. No explanation was satisfactory in his mind.

When he started hitting her, she started screaming at the top of her lungs.

According to the neighbors this was not his first time to physically a buse her. They began to call each other immediately. The ladies got together and instantly knew what to do. They went to the house but the front door was locked. They could hear her husband's angry words and her sobs. The oldest lady went through the back door that was open and the rest of the ladies followed. They circled the surprised man and took the whip from his hand.

The oldest lady we called "Grandma" told him, "Now it is our turn. Get your pants off. We want you to experience what we have to bear with men like you. This has to stop! We are going to make an example of you!"

He dropped on his knees and started crying, begging forgiveness from his wife and asking her to protect him and to not let them hit him.

That was the last time that a man in that community beat his wife.

The ladies could not stop talking about it. They had understood what it is to be "The Body of Christ." They were in solidarity with one another.

The women did not wait for the next meeting but immediately the next day, three of them came to the mission to let us know what they had been able to accomplish. Again, we were overjoyed to see the changes the community was experiencing. As a result they became stronger and were respected by the men, as equal human beings. We talked about the scripture. Woman was to be a partner to man, not a slave, servant, or lower class person; made in God's image and comparable to man.

This was definitely a result of reflecting on God's word and understanding what it entailed to be a good Christian. They began to realize what God wanted of each of them. The Word of God was alive and had fallen into good ground, had taken root, and it was bring forth an abundant harvest. In that community, we built a women's center for them to meet and do their communal activities.

Everything was accomplished with donations of materials from the different institutions, while the community did the labor. Everyone in the community young and old, men, woman and children worked from the very beginning until we were able to celebrate and use the women's center.

A child without a home

It was in this community that I was given the first child while I was ministering there. One of the ladies told me of a grandmother who was dying of cancer. We immediately went to visit her to find out what her needs were.

It was a horror to see where she lived, a 12x 14 room, with only open spaces for windows and doors, some rugs hanging for privacy in the openings. It was built in a swamp so there was flooding all over and the smell was appalling. She lay on top of an old dirty mat surrounded by her grandchildren that were dirty and hungry. It was very evident they had not eaten for a while. Barely able to speak, she told the sad story of her daughter. (See picture #8)

"My daughter is a prostitute. She needs the money to be able to support her children. I really don't know where she is or where she works. Once in a while she comes and brings some food for the children and then she disappears. Her husband's pay is not enough to feed us. Now I am dying, and I can't take care of the children any longer."

She said, "I heard about you, the work you are doing with women. I need your help. Please help me. You were sent by God to me." Because of her illness and the children she had to care for, she was unable to join in the ladies' activities. "Now that the end seems close for me to die, I need to ask you something important." She explained.

"In whatever way I can help," I responded assuring her the best I could.

But I never expected what I was about to hear. The elderly woman slowly brought a paper from her bosom and showed me. The papers were about the oldest granddaughter whom she wanted to give to me. "I don't know anyone else to whom I can entrust her; I have taken care of her since birth.

" Carmen was given to her by her daughter who was then a single mother. The man who is the father of the other children did not want Carmen and grandma was afraid for her. Carmen was legally the grandmother's, and now she wanted to give her to me.

It was hard for me to believe this was happening. I thought of Jesus saying, "Let the children come to me." The child was lying by grandma's head listening to all this conversation. Sitting down closer to both of them, I took the child and held her on my lap and said, "Listen to me, I love you both and I am going to do whatever is best in this circumstance." I could not bring myself to speak further, afraid to make promises I couldn't keep and have them feel let down.

"There is no way that I can take this responsibility," I thought. We prayed for God's guidance and left them with the hope that something would be arranged. I promised to come back as soon as possible. It was one of the hardest home visits I have ever made.

We called an emergency meeting of the women's group. We prayed about what to do and decided that we all needed to help her.

First, two or three women would have to clean the house and area around the house to discourage the mosquitoes which could make all of them sick. Others would take care of the children.

I would go with a couple of ladies to ask for a donation from the city, of Lago Agrio and Texaco Oil Company, and any other institutions. We needed sand, cement, metal for the roof, material for a floor, and to put in the windows and a door. From the mission, we would bring food, a nurse, a bed, a mattress, so that she could be as comfortable as possible in her last days.

The ladies would take turns feeding her and caring for the children. The lack of funds in this community made it an added burden to get money for medicine. The daughter was no where to be found, nor was her husband.

The most difficult part was to explain why I could not take the child with me. A child needed stability and care, and my life could not offer that. I was seldom home. I went from place to place, so I asked if she would allow me to find the child a good home. She agreed to this and wrote a statement to that effect.

I brought up this case to the other missionaries asking them to help me find her a home. They had been there longer and knew more people than I did. We started looking for a family that could afford to take one more child into their home and really love her.

One of the missionaries suggested a lady from Via Colombia who was one of the leaders of their community. I went to visit her and talked to her and her husband about the possibility of taking another child.

She and her husband agreed, even though they already had seven children, both boys and girls. Their answer was, "God will provide."

They had a big home and a good piece of land which they cultivated and raised chickens, pigs, and a couple of cows. (See picture #2) They had working dogs that protected their home.

The day came to take the child to her new home. Carmen was a five-year-old. In her little hands, she carried a dirty old plastic bag with all her positions; one pair of underpants, one raggedy skirt and one blouse.

I had a hard time holding the dam of tears that was building in me. All I could do was embrace the child. I brought her clothes, in the following visits and food to help the family who took her in. I felt responsible. Seeing so much poverty and misery in so many ways was overwhelming at times.

My thoughts went to other places where there was such waste and lack of appreciation for what they had. My prayer was, "God, I know you must see and feel for us, your children. Why is there so much inequality? I surrender. I can't do much. It is devastating for me. Give me strength."

The answer from God was always, "I love you." A great peace would surround me. God never failed me. I was given a peace and had energy to keep going. I could feel God embracing me and felt His consolation that I was doing what I could under the circumstances.

As St. Paul who experienced suffering and trials, I needed to encourage the other believers and not let a tear drop from my eyes. A major concern was to know enough about the Lord, and to explain the hope that was available to them in their daily lives.

I wanted each person to realize they did not have to understand their suffering. Their responsibility was to tell others what God had done for them. My prayer was, *"God prepare me to tell others about the hope I have in you."* I always thought I had received so much and much would be asked of me. So I kept on working.

Teaching was my passion and I desired to let the people know that God had not forgotten them. The care of the grandmother through her illness was very demanding on the community. It took a couple of weeks of extensive care as the ladies took turns until the old woman died. They even took care of the burial and everything else on their own. By then I was in another community.

Later on, we found out the daughter had come to pick up the children, and the ladies invited her to the meetings to hear the Word of God. She was invited to join the group. The community shared with her that they would help her, as they could to care of her children. She only showed up two times and we never saw her again. Carmen's mother never asked me or anyone else for her oldest child.

This was heavy on my heart but I could not dwell on the grief and suffering of all those I met. I had to be ready for the next visit to another community, another reality.

The women with their guides and leaders continued to examine the various Biblical texts about how Jesus treated the women. They were very simple women (some did not even know how to read or write.) But their heart was in the right place.

They had a tremendous amount of wisdom. They had a hunger for God and wanted to understand what God wanted of them. By understanding Jesus' way, they would be ready for any hardships that would come their way. They could teach the young ones the hope in Jesus and what he had done for them.

Picture No. 1 – Riding to Lago Agrio

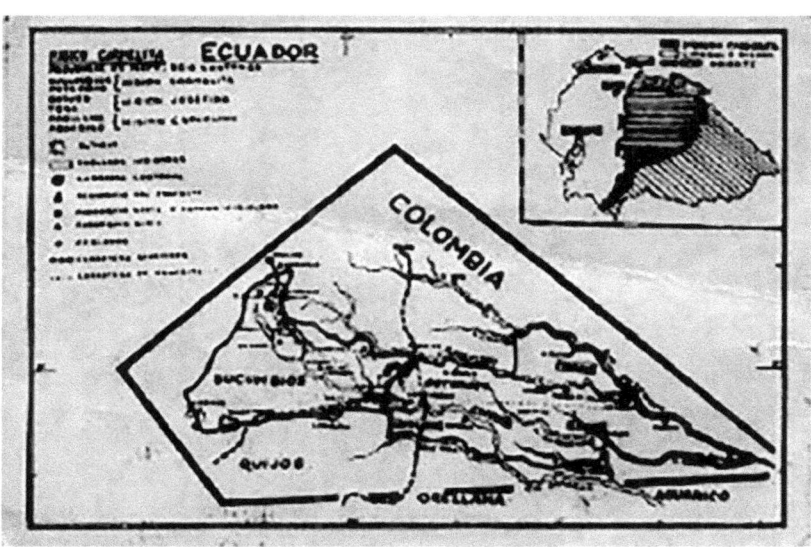

Picture No. 2 – Map of Sucumbios

Picture No. 3 – Crossing Aguarico River

Picture No. 4 – Lago Agrio

Picture No. 5 – Childrens Bible Class

Picture No. 6 – Youth Puppeters

Picture No. 7 – Ferry crossing the river

Picture No. 8 – Orphan girl

Picture No. 9 – Youth Group

Picture No. 10 – Texaco waste

Picture No. 11 – Taking a bath in the polluted river

Picture No. 12 – Moving out of Aguarico

Picture No. 13 – COIM group

Picture No. 14 – Sewing Table

Picture No. 15 – Weeding the Rice

Picture No. 16 – Aguarico

Picture No. 17 – Sister Building a Bench

Picture No. 18 – The Bishop Cooking

Picture No. 19 – The Motorcycle

Picture No. 20 – Celso's Artwork

Picture No. 21 – Building the Church

Picture No. 22 – Music Ministry

Chapter 8

A New Group From and For The Mission

"For God so loved the world that he gave his only Son, so that everyone who believes in him might not perish but might have eternal life."

John 3: 16 (TNAB)

What an opportunity it was for me to do my part in the work Jesus had begun. I felt this project came from God. He wanted me to share, in a very specific way, the work that Jesus did in loving one another and telling the Good News *"That all may have eternal life."* Since November 14, 1980 when I arrived at the mission place, I had been ministering in different areas by evangelizing, teaching, visiting families and communities. I had programs for the youth group, the children, and the adults of The Carmelite Mission.

At the same time, I was praying, searching, and frequently talking with Monsignor Gonzalo Lopez about the dream he had for a local church in the jungle. He wanted me to be a part of that church. A new group dedicated to mission work, from the mission and for the mission... (see picture #9)

March 24, 1981, was the date my commitment was finalized. All the legal arrangements were made with Bishop John Ward from Los Angeles and with the Superior general, head of the SDSH where I belonged before coming to the Mission. The decision was officially communicated by Monsignor Gonzalo Lopez Marañon. "Maria Luisa Jimenez has been accepted and will be staying at the service of *'Sucumbíos Church'* as a missionary in the Church of San

Miguel de Sucumbíos in Ecuador, South America."[3]

According to the notes written by Monsignor Gonzalo and me, the goal was: "To establish a Community of Sisters who would consecrate themselves for life to the local Church." This was officially approved.

Our focus would start with the young people who were interested in knowing and serving Jesus Christ. We had regular visits and monthly weekend youth encounters. The young people came from all the communities around. (See picture #9)

This gave us an opportunity to see who the young leaders were and to determine the possibilities for the local church to grow. We called these gatherings "Youth Encounters" (*Convivencias*).

When it was a week-end encounter, each young person contributed for their training with whatever they had. No fee was required. Some brought bananas, yucca, papayas, or whatever fruit they grew at home. Once in a while, the ones who were economically better off would bring a chicken and some eggs. Everyone was fed and had a place to sleep and enjoy the weekend together.

The focus was on evangelization, Jesus Christ in our lives, and our role in bringing about the kingdom of God. The program was full of games, songs, skits relating real life events and how the Word of God applied to that life.

When we had a one-day seminar, it was not necessary for them to bring food. It was in these groups we started searching for the ones who had potential. Those seemed called to follow this way of life. It was amazing and very fulfilling.

In a letter dated November 1[st,] I wrote to Louise, a friend whom I had invited to come and see our work in the Mission field. She accepted the invitation; later, I learned she wrote her thesis about the missionary project and her adventures at the mission. Here is a portion of what she wrote:

"He (Monsignor Gonzalo) surprised Maria Luisa by asking her not to join the Carmelite Sisters. Monsignor told her that a few native Ecuadorians who had joined the mission staff were content to fall into the roles of supporting the Spanish and Colombian missionaries.
He felt the future of the Church in Ecuador depended on its ability to stand on its own two feet. Monsignor Gonzalo wanted to see natives rising to positions of leadership, not taking backseat positions. For a long time he had dreamed of starting a seminary school and a community for native woman to serve the Diocesan Church. Monsignor Gonzalo told Maria Luisa that he had been praying for the right person to help start such a religious community of native daughters.".4

Visit of Pope John Paul II

Macario was a young man who prospect to become a member of the new group being formed. He wrote: "It was at the Youth encounters I met Maria Luisa and the group. I had been working as a Catechist, a leader in the Communities around Lago Agrio.

I was named the President of the area, and for that reason I was one of the delegates selected to represent the Church when the Pope John Paul II visited Cuenca, Ecuador, December 1984.

From the Sucumbíos Church, there were 30 delegates representing the Catechists, and the Christian Leaders. *(Animadores de la Comunidad.)* Mary and I went from our group. We traveled to Cuenca on a bus a whole day and night. The roads were terrible, but we had fun singing and praising, God for His goodness. We told jokes and our own stories and talked about everyday life's struggles and successes. After an enjoyable trip, we arrived at Cuenca where the organizers had assigned us to sleep in a school classroom. Thank goodness there were bathroom facilities. There was a classroom for the women and a classroom for the men. We were not really prepared for this; the floor was hard and the weather mercilessly bitter cold.

We barely slept and had to get up early in the morning. We prayed the Rosary, and sang while were walking in procession to celebrate Mass with the Pope.

We arrived at 7:00 a.m. The Pope was scheduled to be there at 11:00 a.m. He arrived at 1:00 pm. We ate what we took with us for the trip and some bananas and apples. There wasn't any hot food. The excitement was very high for us all. The people were so numerous; they looked like mountains of ants, there were representatives from every church in Ecuador. Even though we were a group, there was the real possibility of getting lost among the crowd in an unknown city.

Macario was a blessing for me. I had a poncho but because of the number of people and the long walk, I got warm and could barely carry it. He carried it for me and I asked him to stay close by me, which he did. I needed him for protection.

When we got to where we needed to show the tickets to enter, we saw quite a sight. There was a line of military personnel guarding the whole area. People were pushing and pulling trying to get in no matter what. I could barely take out my tickets to show the police at the make-shift gate. Macario pushed me to enable us to move ahead.

Though it was heavily guarded, there were still some people that sneaked in without a ticket.

In Ecuador, the people's devotion to the Pope is significant for Catholics. The Pope is the representative of Christ here on earth, so everyone would like to have a chance to at least see him. Just to touch him, and if possible to get close enough to get his blessing.

Finally we were at the place with names of all the Dioceses of Ecuador and found the sign showing where the Sucumbíos Representatives should be. It was not far from where the celebrants were going to be. It took a long time to organize those thousands of people. While we waited, we were singing, clapping, and praying. In front of us was a huge platform to make sure everyone could see the Pope. We were about sixty feet from the Pope's Chair where he would be celebrating the Eucharist. The Cardinals, Bishops, Monsignors and important priests, were also up on the platform. It was impressive and powerful.

During the worship a wind blew the cups which contained the Hosts. They did not have covers.

According to Catholic belief these wafers would be blessed during Mass and become the Body of Jesus. The wind started to blow the wafers out. I was close so I did my best to try to recover some of them but it was impossible. I could not find anything to cover them with. I signaled some priests to let them know what was happening. The peoples' focus was on the Pope, so they did not realize they were stepping on the Hosts. I thought I might get trampled; I abandoned the effort and let the priests take care of it.

My tiredness from the trip, my poor health, and not having eaten for so long got the best of me. I fell asleep during his preaching. I could not tell you what he talked about. I woke up when the choir started singing.

One of the priest organizers came to let us know that the plan had changed because they were behind schedule. "The Pope will not put the medals or Crosses on each Church representative. There is much danger for him." He asked each head responsible from each church to get the crosses from him, to take back to their own church and have the ceremony there.

He then showed me where he would be giving out the crosses and medals.

When the Mass was over, I had the task of finding the priest who was to give me the crosses and medals. I asked the group to stay where they were and started my walk up to the platform. Without realizing it, I climbed up on the Pope's chair to see if I could find the priest. I did see him and was able to follow him down the steps, around some rooms and doors and finally I obtained the crosses and medals. Coming out was another terrible ordeal. When people saw what I had, they wanted to take the package from me. I had to guard it as if my life depended on it. I told them, pointing in the direction of the priest, "Go ahead you'll get them there."

I ran up the steps unable to hide the package. With God's help I made it. I came out from the darkness to the bright light making me totally disoriented and unable to find our group. I saw now that I could not step on the Pope's Chair or on the altar, so I kept praying and asking God to intervene. I was walking around when Macario came again to my rescue.

I heard him call my name and as I turned I saw our small group and went to them. They were so happy that I had been able to get their crosses and medals.

We flowed out of the place as though we were a river of people. However, it was easier since nothing was stopping us.

We found something to eat and got on the bus to go back home. We had feelings of excitement and relief. It was an unforgettable experience for everyone. Some said they certainly saw Jesus; He was talking to them, let them know He loves them and he had became one of us to save us personally.

Each member had something to tell that was meaningful to them, whether it was during Mass, the procession, or the time of waiting. I was inspired by them and embarrassed to say I felt asleep during his preaching. I let them know how they inspired me and had given me the strength at this time in my journey. We had abundant experiences to tell each community, in the whole Sucumbíos Church which was renewed. We set a date to have the ceremony to give the crosses from the Pope to the ones who were present at the Celebration of the Eucharist at Cuenca.

Some months later at one of the National Conferences, I met leaders of other Churches who were at the event. They said they were never able to get the medals and crosses. They were told a package would be mailed to them, but they never received it. I realized it was a miracle that I was able to get the crosses and medals, I thanked God for them. It meant so much to the people, who were there and they will never forget the experience.

At times, Monsignor Gonzalo would travel from Quito to Lago Agrio. During his visits, I would meet with him regularly to continue working on the development of the project. I took careful notes, even of the seemingly unimportant comments. What was Monsignor's dream for the group? What were his ideas, goals, and steps we needed to follow? I was able to insert my own ideas as to what I saw as a woman with experience and a vision for the future.

It took much time and effort but it showed what was important in Monsignor's mind and heart. As the plan was developing, it needed a lot of time for reflection.

In carrying out his plans, little by little we would start seeing them unfold. It was a hope for the local church to grow and make this church our own.

A Bishop sweeping the floor

One of the discussions and differences in Monsignor Gonzalo's vision and mine came after he stated, "I want a group where the women do what they are most capable of (house work)." I wanted a group where both men and woman would be able to do all kinds of work. Everyone would be responsible for their own self in all the activities. The old idea of the Sisters taking care of the Priests' needs did not appeal to me from the beginning.

I said, "I do not want to have a group of servants for the priests. It will not be God's will according to my understanding of the scripture." We had some great discussions about this. My vision was that all share in the work and does everything as a team, especially when we are in a communal living situation. It would be a new group doing things in a different way and we would be the model.

One week each month Monsignor Gonzalo came to stay with the group. He became a participant and would take a broom sweep the floor or a dish cloth and clean the table. It was modeling the new way that this group would be. A priest thought this was one of the worst things that could happen because he was used to the Sisters care. Change was difficult in the minds of the people there, but it was the beginning of women seeing their own value. Another question we discussed was:

- *What would be the specifics of the group?*

The name the group had been using was changed from "Female vocational group" to "Sisters in Aguarico at the service of the Church of Sucumbíos."

The official commitment day was August 11, 1981. According to Monsignor Gonzalo he wrote: "She (me) is going to be the originator of the new community of Sisters, from and for the Church San Miguel de Sucumbíos." It was on that date I took my vows during a Celebration of the Eucharist. Monsignor Gonzalos wrote in his diary, "Maria Luisa Jiménez vows as Sister of the Sucumbíos Church."

Present at the celebration was Louise, a friend who came to visit me, she wrote:

> 5"I was happy for the warm feeling I had inside because of what was about to happen. Reciting vows has much of the excitement of a wedding. For me to be present now for this private ceremony was like a very special gift from God. I gave her a special cross……. It was the custom to recite your vows while holding a crucifix. Since it was a resurrection crucifix, I felt it symbolized a new life for her and the new community that was forming."6

The new group idea was presented to all the missionaries at the General Assembly of Missionaries in August 1981: "The group is born out of the need to include local people to become permanent leaders at the service of the Church."

I liked that and I thanked God for using me as His instrument of grace for that area. I saw that all my training in the United States had been for a reason and was bearing fruit. I praised God constantly. The vision was clear now. This group would have the three pillars:

1-Identify with the local church.

2-The priorities would be pastoral work and Catechist.

3- Carmelite spirituality.

The Carmelite Sisters who had lived in the house moved to Lago Agrio. The house was left for the new group to be in charge of the hospitality for missionaries and people that needed a place to stay. Louise stayed at this house where two young women, Blanca and Priscilla helped with cooking and washing clothes.

There was much going on, so I asked Louise to accompany me to visit the young women who were possible candidates. I also asked her to prepare Blanca to receive her First Communion. It was very difficult for Louise with the cultural and language barrier, but she gladly did her best and Blanca was able to participate fully in the Body of Christ by receiving Holy Communion with the rest of us.

At this time we had two more women that joined the group, Carmen and Gladys. With them in mind, we started a team. On October 1, 1981 at the feast of St. Therese of Lassie in the house of Puerto Aguarico, we had a special small religious ceremony.

The participants attending the ceremony were many missionaries who worked in the mission at Aguarico Center.

We had planned a three-day retreat directed by Reverend Baranda. He talked about God's call on our life and becoming closer to Him through prayer and contemplation on His Word. After the retreat, the small team now had their responsibilities:

1. To minister to the communities near by

2. To take care of the center as a hospitality house where missionaries, lay personal, or visitors could visit and their needs be met.

    Carmen had a religious-life background and Gladys was our only real local church member. We felt blessed with a young Sister to coach and see what the Spirit would do with her. I have the strong belief that "Life is a journey." God allows us to have some companions on our journey, for a long time and others for a short time. We each need to hear God's voice and follow it.

    Carmen and Gladys did not stay long. They had a different vision and expectation of the group. Others started coming in. It was wonderful to see God working. After this retreat there would be many more that helped us keep our eyes on Jesus.

    Few of the Carmelite Missionaries were not so enthusiastic about the group. A couple of them wondered and verbalized, "Why has Monsignor Gonzalo chosen Maria Luisa to start the group and not one of the Carmelite Sisters who have been working and dedicating their lives for so many years already?" This was the start of a not-so-good feeling, between the natives versus the foreigners.

    It was January 17, 1981 when Monsignor Gonzalo said, "I trust that at the end there will be a triumph of Jesus our Lord in the Local Church. Do not be afraid"[7] He was referring to the problem that was brewing among the missionaries. This group was like a very small seed just starting to grow and needing tender loving care. But it had to be healthy and thriving from the very beginning. It was a great challenge to get the missionaries to help in training the young that were coming in. One by one some were able to overcome their personal prejudices about the group and generously gave us a hand.

The strike

It was at this time when the big oil companies, (Texaco being the main one) were going to build a resort for the foreign workers who were treated royally. The native workers were treated unfairly with poor sleeping accommodations and never enough food to eat. It was hard to understand the double standards. They left waste oil in large standing ponds, with no regard for the environment and water supplies. (see picture #10) The oil seeped into the river. This was the water supply for both people and animals for drinking and bathing. (see picture #11) The workers decided to go on strike.

Monsignor Gonzalo listened, at a meeting, to the facts expressed by Reverend Gallegos who had been ministering to the workers. Monsignor Gonzalo also heard comments from other missionaries who had received information from the workers. After hearing the issues and praying, he expressed his views. "It is a question of justice for the poor; we are the voice of the poor. We want to support them." He also let everyone decide where they would stand on this issue.

After that meeting, the ladies group met. I let them know what a serious decision this was and the possible dangerous outcomes. I informed them we were going to pray and think. They would have a choice to go home and come back when the strike was over if they felt they could not be a part of an activity of such dimensions, or they could stay and support the strikers. We cancelled all our activities in the communities to support the workers on their strike.

Everyone mutually agreed to stay and help.

It was my first group experience. I felt responsible if anything happened to them. We prayed and decided we would make ourselves available for whatever was needed. I was afraid for the young Sisters, but was very excited that they wanted to join in the strike and help. I was doing what Jesus did by putting my life on the line. I was on high energy the first day and I had no idea how long this strike would last.

My job was to drive a truck to take food to the men on strike. A team of women and men went with me to help deliver it. There were big containers of soup, rice, and beans with sometimes a little piece of meat. We gave them a drink of water and occasionally added sweetness and lemon in it. The sisters helped in the kitchen. In the afternoon we gathered with the main group at the Texaco Company gate. We prayed with the strikers, read a little from the Bible, had a short reflection and sang, for and with them. We had copies of the words of the songs. So they could sing with us. I played the guitar. To encourage one another we used the songs.

Some songs were words made up by the people and put to the tune of our own folk music. As the days passed and there was no resolution to the strike, my energy and enthusiasm were withering. What kept me going was the thought that every night I could take a shower and go to bed. The men on strike had to stay, on their post rain or shine, having no showers, no accommodations, and no rest. My whole body ached for more sleep and rest but we had to get up, pray and go on the next day. It was our first experience of taking the side of the poor as a group in such a public forum. We were being prepared for many more dangerous ones to come.

The days went very slowly and sometimes we thought time stood still. The heat and mosquitoes were unbearable along with the rain and the mud all around. Yet, we kept going because of our commitment and conviction that God wanted us to be there. People came from all around; the military were in control now. They said they were protecting the "interest of the country" but it was clear that they were actually protecting the interest of the companies that were drilling for petroleum.

The Military takes our Priest

On one of the days of the strike, the military took Reverend Gallegos (the Priest who ministered to the strikers) saying, "He is the trouble maker and getting the people aroused." When we saw that Reverend Gallegos was taken in a military car, Monsignor Gonzalo told me to follow them. That was all I needed to hear. Some women and I jumped into an open truck and told the driver not to lose the car that was taking the Priest Gallegos.

When we arrived at the military zone, where the cars could not go any farther, we jumped down to follow on foot. A mob had gathered. We had to push very strongly against the people to be able to make room to follow the Priest. I put my head down and pushed with my shoulder. Those following were doing the same. I bumped into something and could go no farther. I opened my eyes and saw green boots. Slowly I lifted my head and saw a rifle pointing at me.

A man's voice said, "Don't move one more step."

I froze, opened my arms, and held the other ladies back and we huddled together. We started talking fast. I told him, "We only wanted to make sure the Priest did not get shot or abused. We wanted to make sure he is all right. We are unarmed. We mean no harm. We were sent by the Bishop."

The military asked, "Who are you?"

I said, "I am Sister Maria Luisa Jimenez. We didn't carry our ID."

"Where are you from?" he asked.

I said, "I am from Borja, Canton Quijos."

He said, "You are not, you have an accent."

I replied, "I have been out of the country. Ask me anything, geography or history. I'll show you I am from here." I told him about my family.

He said; "Why do you think the Priest is going to be hurt?"

I answered, "There have been many Priests who already had been killed. I read about it in the newspaper. We don't want this to happen to him."

Then he said, "If you are a Sister, you should be in the church praying. What are doing here?" The ladies spoke up at this time. Bravely they said almost in a chorus, "We are the Church. She is doing her duty right here with us. We are praying, and we are standing to take care of our Priest.

He said, "He is a foreigner. All these foreigners are arousing the people. They are communist."

Someone from the crowd shouted, "You said that just to have an excuse to kill him."

"Shut up!" the military hollered.

All this time the rifle was still pointed at me. Trembling, I asked him to point downward and he did so. I regained my strength to speak again. He is not a communist I said. I had the nerve now to ask, "Where is your captain?"

He said. "I am the captain."

So I humbly said, "Captain, if I were your mother, if I was your sister, would you kill me?"

He said, "Why are you saying that."

I replied, "Because I know in some places many innocent people already have died. Before you make a decision to shoot us, I want you to think, 'I am going to kill my mother or my sister.' We are brothers and sisters. We want what is best for all. Please Captain, do think about it. Let us just be here and watch and pray. We mean no harm." He seemed to relax. We were experiencing a miracle.

He then said, "Alright! Just don't make any more trouble!

We started praying the Rosary out loud.

He called a soldier and told him something and a little later, he brought some drinks to all of us. Looking through the glass windows of the building where Reverend Gallegos was held, we could see him animatedly moving his hands and talking with the general. We decided, "The danger has passed."

I don't know how long we stayed but being crowded together in the heat of the day made us perspire very much. Our fear was leaving us. All the rifles were down now, yet at times I felt like fainting. I called on God, the Deliverer who sustained me. At last they freed Reverend Gallegos.

We went back to the strike line and to the duties of supporting the strikers. I played my guitar and we sang with them. After we had been doing this for many days, we gave copies of the songs to the soldiers. As they became familiar with the songs, some joined in the singing while others kept the tempo with their weapons. We had so much to thank God for. Definitely God was at work! We were being God's instruments and giving our lives at that moment.

We were being Jesus for the workers. We praised God that day as never before. We praised him for his hand of protection on us and Reverend Gallegos. God is our stronghold and our hope. He hears the cries of the poor.

The next day, when the alarm clock went off, it was too soon. Our bodies refused to move. Every muscle and bone in my body was aching. I had no energy. We prayed and prayed that God would intervene to stop the strike. We had little or no enthusiasm to give any more. The cross we were carrying was very heavy. In the meantime, we had our daily chores to do. We had animals to feed; our chickens, the dogs and cats. They could not be left alone.

As the days went on, more people found out we were part of the strike and came to join us. The women's group from Aguarico particularly took turns and came to help. It was a time of solidarity. The strike lasted a very long time, twenty one days. I never realized how much energy, suffering, and pain goes into strikes.

Monsignor Gonzalo is ill

On August 23, 1981, during the Eucharistic celebration, Monsignor Gonzalo fainted. It was the beginning of great changes for the group. His illness took him away to the

United States and Canada for two long years. In his absence, he left Reverend Arroyo and the Vicar Reverend Camarero to support the group.

Monsignor Gonzalo's absence brought about positive and negative outcomes. He had telephone conferences with me a couple of times a month. He encouraged me to continue to do what God had started, with or without him. When I expressed my worries, he would say, "Let God takes care of it." Reverend Camarero was now in charge in his absence. Reverend Arroyo was a treasured support person for the group.

On January 11, 1983, we had another retreat with Reverend Jaramillo where he help us to reflect on God, our answer to Him, prayer, and the meaning of Holiness. On March 15, 1983 Reverend Rendueles gave us a retreat; on the reason to be faithful to Jesus, grace our goals. Jesus is the one who was sent.

One of the elders of the Sucumbíos Church was Reverend Rendueles. He had been with the Carmelites since 1958, in Quito, Guayaquil and Sucumbíos in Ecuador. 8

In 1972-73 Reverend Cantero joined, The Carmelite Mission.9 He had worked in Palma Roja, Los Rios, Putumayo, and Aguarico. In 1983 a retreat was held, directed by this humble yet very spiritual Carmelite Priest. He had experience and knew Sucumbíos very well. The retreat covered:

• Jesus the Visible Sacrament of God.

• God's plan for us.

This was preparing us for the next step ahead and giving us a better idea of God's plan for us. The group was changing more and we moved to another community to live as the poor people lived, "The poor living with the poor."

On September 20, 1983 during the Celebration of the Eucharist in the Cathedral of Lago Agrio, with her family and all the parishioners, Elida made her official promise and joined the group. Her celebration was done at the Community 10 of August. She was a product of those Youth Encounters.

From the first meeting I had with her, I could sense this young woman had a great desire for God. In this group, her talents were generously shared. She was one of the pillars of the group in a quiet way. Many times she reminded me of Saint Therese "The little Flower." She did small things with great love.

Chapter 9

Living Out Our Commitment For The Poor

"Not everyone who says to Me, "Lord Lord", shall enter the kingdom of heaven, but he who does the will of my Father in heaven."

Matt. 7:21 (TNAB)

The name of the community where we moved to was called *"Diez De Agosto."* The certainty and conviction that we're doing God's will kept us going. The ideas of the group were developing about what we should do, and where and how we should live. It was decided the group should not live at a mission center but live as a community the way poor people do. At first we called ourselves the Ladies Vocational group, then *Sisters of the Sucumbíos Church*. Now it was called Communities for the Church and the World. *"Comunidades para la Iglesia y el Mundo."* (COIM.)

Monsignor Gonzalo made arrangements with a member of that community Mr. Ortiz offered us a place to stay in his future home. The home was not finished, he was still working on. This would be our temporary home until we could find a permanent place.

We talked with the rest of the group about this arrangement and decided to take just our personal belongings with us when we moved.

The anticipated day for moving came for our group composed of Elida, Isabel, Mary, and I. We were given the blue Toyota truck that I had been driving since I arrived at the Mission from the United States. Monsignor Gonzalo and

Clever were present to see us off.(See picture #12)

We traveled on a dirt road to get to the community. (Many times in the winter, we had to push the truck because it would not go over the ditches. In the summertime it was OK to drive.) We loaded our personal belongings, my guitar, books and a couple of pots and pans. Also we took nine chickens and one rooster to start a flock to provide meat and eggs for our survival. It only took one trip to carry everything.

The books took up the most space. We needed them for the training and formation of the group. We had Bibles, the book of Christian prayer, books on spirituality, contemplation, lives of the Saints and psychology, etc.

This community we were moving to was one that had already been worked by missionaries. It was well organized. When a missionary came for a regular visit, the people would meet at the school building.

The house we were to live in was a wooden, two-story building. The frame and the roof were completed. On the second floor some floor boards about ten inches wide, an inch thick and eighteen feet long were lying in place on beams but not nailed down. Only one room on the second floor had all four walls enclosed. It had a cut-out space for a future window that faced the plaza and a space for one inside door. Fortunately, the floor was nailed down it that room. We found something to hang over the window and door. We four Sisters lived in that room.

There was a wooden ladder we used to get to our room. At night it became a life and death challenge to go up or down it. The trick was to walk on the floor to our room without stepping off the end of a loose plank and falling to our death on the first floor. It seemed like forever before the rest of the floor was securely nailed.

It was early in the afternoon when we arrived at the community. The first thing we had to do was take care of the chickens, which were lying on their sides because their feet were tied together. We untied one foot and left the string on the other foot so we could fasten it to a log by the kitchen. That way the chickens could not run away.

We unloaded the truck and started looking for places to put things away. We placed the books outside of one of the corner bedroom walls. A temporary kitchen was set up on the first floor on the ground between the beams across the floor. We built a place to cook by putting down some big rocks about three feet apart and then laid three iron rods over them to set pots on. Gathering firewood was necessary while it was still daylight.

It took a while for the chickens to get used to the new surroundings. We fed them corn and gave them water. Later after two days, little by little, we freed them to go out into the field and run through the coffee plantation searching for worms. There was a tree near the house.

After a couple of days, the chickens started flying up to the limbs for shelter and to sleep at night. Even the chickens had to adjust to their new way of life, as all the other chickens in the area had. They no longer had an enclosed protective chicken coop. They were part of the COIM group. They were very important because we were counting on them for eggs and meat.

Since there was no electricity, we used a diesel lamp; no running water meant we would have to carry it from the river, a couple of blocks away. We made sure we took care of the basic necessities while the sun was shining. After we ate and washed the dishes, it was time to pray. There was much to be thankful for. It was also time to reflect on what we were going through at this time. For us, it was doing God's will. It had come directly from the Bishop. We were the "dream come true" for him to have a group from the Mission for the local church in Sucumbíos.

That night, our evening prayers and our singing were very meaningful. It helped to know many Psalms, some of encouragement in time of trials, some for when we were afraid, and others for protection.

We thanked God for this new start. We made a list of what we needed to do the next day. Our goals were to continue settling in and bringing order to our living accommodations. We would settle in, a little at a time. We must talk to the neighbors and let them know we were there to stay and that we would need to find a permanent home. Our being there was not just a visit. Some already surmised this when they saw the truck come in and unload.

A four-year-old cooks for the family

One of our neighbors was a rooster fighting gambler. He had expensive roosters which were fed better than his children. I went to visit the family mid-morning. I found a four-year old girl, who was about to cook a big pot of green bananas. Her mom and dad had gone to plant some coffee plants. She said she had to have the food ready for them when they came back from work. She also had to baby sit her younger brother and sister.

Seeing the little ones so dirty and barely clothed made me feel like crying.

There was very little I could do, but I could help her peel the bananas, set the pot on the fire and wash the faces of the little ones. At any time one of the children could have fallen into the fire or gotten scalded by the water that was almost ready for boiling the bananas. Just thinking about it was scary for me. My fear was real because it had happened to me; I still have the scars on my right hand. There wasn't one toy for them to play with. They were playing on the dirt floor with a short stick.

I decided to tell them a short story about Jesus. The children loved it. I could not help comparing the differences between my childhood and theirs. The responsibility this child had at four years old was too great. She was doing a woman's job.

I had my mother and older sisters to look after me. I had chores to do but never had to cook or be completely responsible for the younger ones. I realized how blessed I had been and had taken it for granted, until I saw this child in these circumstances.

Washing our clothes

The group was growing in numbers and in wisdom. When we visited the families we went by twos, like the disciples. We found out the ladies washed clothes and took their baths at the river, which was not too far from our home. We carried water to the house in buckets, to wash dishes and cook. We carried our dirty clothes to the river, washed them, took a bath, and walked back home with the clean wet clothes. There we hung them up or draped them over bushes to dry. Thinking back, I don't know how we did it.

A tree had fallen by the river and one of the big branches was lying perfectly across it, to be used as a table, on which we scrubbed the clothes. The jeans were the hardest to wash because the material is stiff and the mud does not easily come out. My hands and knuckles hurt and at times were bleeding until I grew calluses and learned how to scrub.

When I was at the Mission Center in Aguarico I did not have to worry about washing clothes because we had young women who did these chores for us. They also washed the priests' clothes and jeans.

For me it was a big change but for the young women in the communities around who had joined the group I could see it was not a big deal. It was part of their normal life from an early age.

The owner of our house would often come after work to put a few nails on the floor to secure it and to start work on enclosing another room. But darkness came soon so he couldn't do much. We felt it was dangerous for us to keep living like this. Everyone else was building and working on their family farms. It was a long time before the people in the community came to help us.

The first thing we needed was an outhouse, so we would not have to go find bushes to hide behind every time nature called. A huge tree five feet, or more across had fallen by the side of the house. I thought if they cut across the tree making five foot circular slabs, three to four inches thick, they could be used for three of the walls. Plastic could be hung across the fourth side for the door. The sides would be kept up by putting sticks in the ground at the base of the three slabs, inside and out. Everyone thought it was a good idea.

The first accident

Some of the men dug a hole about 9 feet deep (that would last a while). Others made a floor over the top of it by placing bamboo down going north and south, then another layer going east and west, except for leaving a hole in the middle. We would squat over the hole when using the outhouse. The toilet paper was a square cut from a newspaper we'd bought in town. The squares were put on a stick and we were allowed one piece each time, more if really needed.

The big round slabs had to be rolled to their places around the floor and hole. All of us were helping. One of the big walls fell on Elida's foot. It was dreadful to see the pain in her face. This was the first accident we had in the process. There would be more, it was a part of life there. I felt responsible for everything that was happening since it was my idea to begin with.

Mr. Ortiz, the town healer, was one of the helpers. He rapidly massaged her ankle and said it was dislocated. He tied it with some rags. That was his first aid.

He wanted to take good care of her, so he found some herbs in the forest and ground them between two rocks and put them as a patch on her ankle. He knew which plants were good for keeping the inflammation down and told her not to walk on it for a couple of days.

Elida was a wonderful hard worker, a beautiful, humble spiritual person. She always reassured me that she was fine even though I could see the pain in her face. She did a lot of helping when she was supposed to be resting her foot.

The days passed quickly as we busied ourselves trying to make our house into a beautiful home. We prayed a lot, read the Bible and "St. Theresa of Avila's Life" which seemed to fit us. The story goes that on a rainy night when Sister Theresa was on her way in a carriage to visit one of the convents she had opened, the carriage wheel broke. The horse stopped. Sister Theresa stepped of the carriage to check the damage to see whether she could continue her trip. When she saw the broken wheel, she raised her hand and shouted to God, "That is why you have so few friends."

On another occasion, it was my turn to get hurt. I was trying to help but I could not pull my hand away fast enough when a beam fell on my little finger. Even though it was not a big thing it was very painful. My small right finger hurt so much I could not stand the healer rubbing and trying to put it back in place. I didn't cry, but I did moan and groan because of the pain. To this day my finger is crooked, and has rheumatoid arthritis in it. Sometimes my finger reminds me of those days as a missionary.

We took turns visiting other communities, and doing our apostolic work of evangelizing. Some had to stay home to care for the chickens. The family man in the community usually hunts, for meat for his family but we had no hunter.

We were young and had a good attitude towards taking this mission, as a wonderful opportunity to show our love for Jesus. It was quite an adventure for me. I was very happy even though I did not have the comforts of home such as a shower. We had to bathe in the river. It was an all-day engagement, plus it was quite a show for all the children and neighbors.

Soon I had to do what every woman there did. I gave up using my bathing suit and began bathing with all my clothes on. I washed my clothes and body at the same time. I put soap on my clothes and rubbed them to get them clean. When I arrived home, I changed into dry clean clothes.

I felt far from life in the United States with all its privacy and comfort, the medicine and the doctor's help, at the tip of my finger; it had all been taken for granted. I especially missed the privacy of a shower and my own room and bed. I knew I was doing what God had called me to do. That kept me enthusiastic and enjoying every minute of every new experience. However, that did not entirely take away the pain of missing the familiar comforts.

Building a shower

My mind conceived an ingenious idea of how to build a private shower and we did it. We collected rain water from the roof of the house, by making bamboo gutters run past the corner of the house, to empty into a big barrel. A faucet was attached to the bottom of the barrel and it worked perfectly.

The community helped again in this undertaking. We used bamboo for the floor so the water would drain down easily into a hole. The four corners were made from large bamboo sticks and we put plastic around for walls. It took a very short time to make.

One hot day after returning home from a long visit to a community, I went straight to the shower. I undressed myself and turned on the faucet. Oh, so refreshing. I surely needed it. Suddenly the weather changed. A strong puff of wind came and instantly blew the walls up. There I was standing perfectly naked. I curled myself into a fetal position and yelled. "Help, help, bring me a towel!"

The neighbors were close enough, that they could have heard my calls. I imagined they were watching from their bamboo home. Besides, I was scared! It felt like a big tropical storm that could carry me away!

Mary came to my rescue and covered me and shut off the faucet. We had a good laugh afterwards.

To make sure it did not happen to anyone else, we fastened the plastic sides with vines. Of course the young Sisters reminded me, "That it is the reason we all take a shower with our clothes on. You never know what might happen!" It was another lesson for me.

During this time, my father decided to pay me a surprise visit. He expressed, very clearly and emphatically, his unhappiness and disagreement with the type of life I had chosen. It was painful to hear him and even worse to see him cry. He said, "I never thought my daughter would come to this. The chickens at the mission center live in better conditions. Why are you doing this? Why do you need to be like this? I am going to talk to the Bishop. There is something very wrong here."

I assured him there was nothing wrong. I had chosen to live as Jesus did, live poor with the poor. We talked for a long time. He refused to accept even a drink of water. He left very sad. It hurt me; I had always hoped my dad would understand how much I loved God and wanted to do what His will. The young Sisters console me and prayed with me.

Well, this was not the end of it. My father convinced my oldest brother Aurelio to come to see me. He wanted me to leave the community I was with and go back to the United States. I was ready for another long discussion with my brother.

He walked around the house and saw how we were living. He said, "Negrita." (Dearest dark one) That was an endearing name he had called me since I was little, when he wanted to make a point, "Don't you think the plastic walls for the shower will fly away with a strong wind"?

I told him, "Oh yes that already happened to me!" He laughed, and ate what we offered him.

He said, "I have come to take you home. It is the wish of our Dad to make you change your mind about living poor with the poor. I do not understand why you want to do this, after living in the United States. Then father was proud and told the neighbors and everyone who knew you how well you were doing in the States. Now you have come back to this? In his words, 'She must be crazy, or want to die young."

My brother finally ended by saying. "If this is the way you want to live, it is up to you." He reminded me that, dad was very sad and disappointed. He can't get over the fact, that you came back to live in misery in this horrible situation."

I reminded my brother that Jesus said to leave mother and father and if we cannot do that we would not be worthy of Him. While I was talking to my brother I was praying for the right words to help my family accept my decision of living poor with the poor. I had to remember:

In the same way, the Spirit too comes to the aid of our weakness: for we do not know how to pray, as we ought, but the Spirit himself intercedes with inexpressible groaning. Romans 8: 26. (TNAB)

The Spirit has always come to my aid and this time was no different. My brother left with the promise try to help change my father's attitude.

Another community member offered us a larger house to use for meetings when Monsignor Gonzalo, came to visit and stay with the group. Those were very amazingly full days. We had to take advantage of his presence. He radiated peace, tranquility, and love.

He had said to me that he would take care of the spirituality of the group. My job was to train teach evangelization, catechesis, and how to practice real Christian living. When we shared the difficult experiences, we had gone though, he would say, "Those are the Communities for the Church and the World. "

The raccoon and the chickens

One night we heard our chickens cackling excitedly. We went outside with a candle, made some loud noises, and then went back to bed. There was nothing we could see, but the chickens were certainly afraid. We went through that routine a couple more times during the night. Once we woke up our neighbor, with the noise we had made.

Early the next morning, we saw what had been going on during the night. It was like a war zone for the chickens. We followed the feathers to where a raccoon had hidden them. He had killed all except two young chickens, we found curled up under a log. We were devastated! It was such a loss for us. Some chickens were still warm from the slaughter.

Several of us started to clean and cut them up to make chicken soup. Others went to let the neighbors know what had happened and to invite them to come and share our large quantity of chicken soup. A couple of ladies came to help. We fed chicken to the community but we had lost our wealth.

At prayer time, we remembered the scripture, "Look at the birds in the sky, the flowers in the fields, they do not sow nor reap but our heavenly Father knows their needs and takes care of them." How could we doubt that He would care of us now?

The next day our neighbor said, "That raccoon knows he did not finish the job. He will come back tonight. I am going to watch for him and kill him." He was concerned about his chickens also. I saw the neighbor late at night sitting with his rifle ready. He had a hunting dog by his side. At his advice, we put one of the dead chickens in a tree as bait where the raccoon wouldn't miss seeing it. At two in the morning, we heard a shot and the dog barking. The raccoon had been killed! The community was grateful to the hunter.

We were told a raccoon becomes an enemy that does not go away until he finishes all the chickens in the area.

Reverend Camarero had told me early in my life at the Mission, "Maria Luisa, we live on the unexpected. We never know what will happen next. We just have to go with the flow and deal with whatever comes to our plate." I was finding out through experience how true those words were. The first weeks and months in that house were very eventful.

The storm in the night

The following happened every time a storm would come, until the walls and windows were installed on the second floor. At night, when a storm came in suddenly, the books and other belongings which had been placed outside of our bedroom against one of two available walls would get wet, if the storm was blowing toward that side. We would scramble out of bed and hurriedly grab the books and stuff and move them to a dry area.

The funny part was, when we were free to go back to bed, the wind might change directions. Then we would literally jump out of bed to find another dry place to put them. There was no room to get all those things, with us inside our bedroom. So we would spend the night trying to care for the books, etc. It almost became a ritual, and we became experts at moving things around quickly. Sometimes the winds and the rain would win and our efforts were futile.

The thought came to mind, "Maybe it would be better not to have anything. That way we would not have to worry." But I believed we needed those books for the formation and education of the group. For me they were a treasure we had to protect. Later on I realized those trials were from God. He wanted us to focus just on God and no one else. He is a jealous God. He will provide. He was preparing us for something greater than the storm and the raccoons.

We looked back at the notes taken at the retreat Reverend Eugenio had given us at the beginning of the group. It was a reminder of why we were there. "Christ is counting on us.

This work at the local church is important to God."

By then the second floor was almost finished except for windows and doors. At this time a couple with their baby came to live with us. They stayed in the second room that was enclosed. We all took turns caring for the baby. This was only for a while, and then they left. Only women were living at the home, at first. When the couple joined us plus two young men, the mix made for difficulties. We tried hard to get along because of our desire to serve God.

For example, after we returned home from Lago Agrio with a truck of supplies, one of the men was upstairs just looking at us smiling, yet he did not come down to help unload the truck. For me this lack of helpfulness was a sign that he did not have what it takes to be a dedicated COIM. There were several other events the group noticed showing he was there "for the ride" and not to serve God and others. Soon after that he left the group.

We prayed continually for a place of our own. The opportunity kept evading us. Whenever there was a possibility, something stopped it, God's answer to our prayers was, "Just wait and be still."

It was surely hard to wait. That has been a frustration all my life. I like things to be done quickly, once I get an idea. Every time, it does not happen right away we thought, God kept us waiting. There was a lesson to learn. We knew in the end it was for the best and God surprises us every time with generosity and love.

Lent is a special time for Catholics. The week before the celebration of the Resurrection, we take time to meditate and have special ceremonies and rituals that help us understand the meaning of God's Word. At this one time I realized how much people understood and took seriously the reflection on the suffering of Jesus on Good Friday. In the Catholic Church we have the custom to pray what is called, "The three hours." We meditate on the seven sayings Jesus spoke before he died. The focus is in reconciliation and conversion as a response to Jesus. We also prepare for the Vigil of the next day.

I suggested that each one of us bring a stick, representing our sins to put on the fire. We planned the fire for Saturday, the blessing of the light.

Each participant at the ceremony would show that "They are repentant and ask forgiveness, of their sins." It is like those sticks burning and disappearing in ashes. We do not have to worry anymore because we are forgiven, "Jesus took our sins upon Himself."

As we were preparing the fire, people started coming from different corners of the plaza bringing their sticks, most of them small. One man about thirty years old was different. He brought an almost tree-size branch. He placed it on the burning fire and said out loud, "God I am sorry for my many sins I promise I will not do them again. I will come to the community meetings and do what You, want me to do."

The people were happily surprised and amazed at the unexpected words from this man. He had humbled himself by publicly acknowledging his sins and demonstrated the enormity of his sins by the size of the branch he brought. He had been a popular man of the night. A woman expressed how she thought about bringing a big stick but thought. "What will the other people think?" So, she brought a small one.

This man was a good example to the rest of the community. He grew taller in everyone's eyes during this ceremony. We all celebrated and talked about his testimony afterwards. He said, "Jesus was raised, and I feel like I am too." We all did that Saturday." It was the best Easter Vigil Celebration we had in that community.

A single mother's fights her abuser

During one of the prayer meetings, a lady was sobbing all the way through and did not look good at all. Afterwards, I put my hand on her shoulder. She stayed behind waiting for everyone to leave before she talked to me. She had a five year old with her. Sensing what was probably coming, one of the Sisters took the child to play. The lady was ready to talk. I asked, "What has happened? Can I help?"

She asked for prayers for strength, saying she is a single mother who lives with her father on her land far from a town. "A couple of days ago, I was going to get the calves away from the mothers so that I could get the much needed milk the next day. There is an old man who has been after me for a while now.

He does not live far from my place. I am afraid of him and prayed to God to protect me. Yesterday on my way back home after taking care of the calves, he was waiting for me. I had a machete in my hand for protection but he immediately was able to overpower me and took it away from me. My son was crying and telling him; 'Leave my mom alone!' he kicked my child and told me, 'You are not going to get away from me now.'"

Her tears were rolling down and I was just holding her. She was shaking, I could feel her fear. Then she continued, "With the help of my son it took a long time before the man had me under him on the grass. I was determined he was not going to have his way. I held on to the long grass behind my head, and dragged myself. He had to get his pants off, so with him getting distracted I had a chance to pull myself up and up. My son kept biting his leg and crying. I kept moving myself away, he could not keep me still. He pulled my underpants off. I kept struggling until he was worn-out. He pushed me aside and kicked me saying, "You are not worth it." And he left.

"I hugged my son dearly, but he had already seen too much," she said. "I thanked God because he gave me the strength to fight to the end. I did not want to get pregnant another time in the same way." I was at a loss for words. We sat on the steps of the school in utter silence and shock. My mind was thinking of the dangers the four of us woman face in this jungle. Only God was our Protector.

Finally when words came to my mind, I asked, "What would you like to do?" "I don't know," she said. "Pray for me." We prayed for strength and wisdom. I asked her if it would be all right for me to tell the priest. Then when he talks to the men he will be able to help stop such terrible abuse.

She did not want me to do anything. She said, "I am too embarrassed." I felt for her, for the child, and my helplessness on knowing what to do. I explained to her that it was not her fault. This was a godless man. What he had done was totally wrong I assured her again it was not her fault.

She told me she had to think about it. She was able to recognize that she had stopped him. He did not get his way, and he probably felt humiliated. But he might try again. We needed a men's organization from the Christian community to educate and protect the women and children. It was the priest's job to get through to those sinful men's hearts and consciences.

We took the lady and her son to our home and offered her some tea to calm her nerves. She said the reason she did not want us to do anything more was because her father is old and would try to kill that man, and he could get killed himself. She did not want that to happen. She needed her father alive. In the future she may tell the priest herself.

We understood that and promised to keep praying for her and her family. The help had to come from our powerful God. We prayed with her specifically now. When she felt better and reassured, she went home. The words of St. Paul came to mind.

> "My God will fully supply whatever you need, in accordance with his glorious riches in Christ Jesus."
>
> *Philippians 4:19 (TNAB)*

Our God certainly was supplying for our group. Young men started to join in our group. The Bishop had changed definitely his idea by now. We will not be a group of Sisters only, but of men, woman and couples. It was a great challenge coming in front of us. God was supplying what was needed when was needed…(see picture #13)

Chapter 10

The Women Find Their Power

"Jesus journeyed from one town and village to another preaching and proclaiming the good news of the kingdom of God. Accompanying him were the twelve and some women who had been cured of evil spirits and infirmities."

(Luke 8:1-2 TNAB)

After having visited all the centers, groups, and organizations in each community of the Sucumbíos Church I had more work to do. I was named as head of the "Women's Department" by Monsignor Gonzalo, who along with his council, had decided that the job would be good for me. By this time, I knew more about some communities than I did about others. I understood the process of building a Base Christian Community and the time it took for the organization to develop a pattern and follow it.

There were thirteen communities where I led women's groups and worked very closely with them. The needs of each community were similar, but there were also some differences, according to where the group lived.

It depended on where they came from, how long they had lived in that place and where each was in their spiritual development. Each person matures differently, so does every group. Each group worked in various sessions, seminars, and conferences in order to set their own goals.

The women's struggles, personal drawbacks, lack of education and finances made the rate of progress uncertain at times. We had general goals and also individual group goals. At the women's meetings, we synthesized the ideas.

How to be able to proclaim the good news of Jesus in this area was the question. We needed to have plans. It was a communal effort that took time to clarify. The following goals were set using ideas from the different groups' efforts and were expressed in this way:

1. To examine Biblical texts about women and Jesus from the woman's perspective. To understand the struggles and personal needs of each woman while accepting the liberation that Jesus brought us.

2. To reflect on the woman's situation in the church and specifically in the Latin-American society, in the light of the Word and our experiences as women.

The Documents of Vatican II, # 4 on "Spirituality of Lay people," when referring to lay people says: *"this lay spirituality wills its particular character from the circumstances of one's state of life'* (married, family life, celibacy, widowhood.) 'Each one has received suitable talents and these should be cultivated as should also the person received from the Holy Spirit."

3. To create an atmosphere of trust in which we would be able to share our struggles and our needs as women and pray together.

4. The church must be 'the salt of the earth' and 'the light of the world." Mt. 5:13-14 (TNAB)

The church is even more urgently called upon to save and renew every creature, so that all things might be restored in Christ, in Him men might form one family and one people of God.

The women would come out in awe after these reflections. They were ready and willing to work on renewing themselves, as well as their family, their community and society. They were ready to make a difference.

5. *To reflect on Mary, the mother of Jesus, a strong, intelligent, practical, disciple full of faith and our model to follow.*

Mary knew how to listen; she was open to God's project. It is a call that demanded a personal response. (Luke 1: 26-38) In her Magnificat she expressed the two fidelities that also give a mark to our own vocation as women.

• *Faithfulness to God and to his project of mercy and love.*

• *Faithfulness to God's people.*

As Catholics the vision we had of Mary the mother of Jesus was almost out of reach for us. That started to change as we saw her as a real human being. The prayers in the litany we said during the Rosary began to tell the story of women. Some examples of the litany we prayed in the past were: Mystic Rose, Tower of David, etc. It was difficult to relate to a person with the adjectives used in the litanies. We said our prayers in a new way: "She was and is:" Mother of the afflicted, mother of the poor, mother of the prostitute, mother of the homeless, mother of the incarcerated, mother of the orphans, etc. These were the people's everyday concerns. Now these women could relate to Mary, the Mother of Jesus, in a practical way.

In some of the celebrations, the women prayed themselves to Mary in their own words.

It was very rewarding to see how the Gospel was being understood in a new way and was coming to life for each one of them. Because of that understanding, and the devotion of the women as a group, God granted many miracles for the whole community. The more the women attended their regular meetings learning from the Word of God, the more their thirst for understanding themselves, the world and God increased. The women were growing.

During the sharing in a meeting, one of them reflected, "I feel like scales have fallen from my eyes. I am reading the Bible in a different way now and I even explain what Jesus is saying to my husband." Everyone clapped, and asked what new passages she had found. How had she done this if she does not know how to read? The woman told us that her daughter was a good reader and was helping the family by reading to them.

"Indeed, the Word of God is living and effective, sharper than any two-edged sword, penetrating even between soul and spirit, joints and marrow and able to discern reflections and thoughts of the heart."

Heb. 4:12 (TNAB)

In addition to my thirteen groups, I had to visit other communities where other teams were working. I would visit each one of them and follow the process with them. Training the leadership was the most important part, requiring much energy and time, but it was a worth the effort. The seeds were falling on good soil and giving forth a hundred fold.

The secret of women success

During this ministry, I found more unexpected realities that women had to face. Slowly each discovered that they found strength in their faith together through their struggles and realized their dreams of solutions. This reality was seen in the experience of the women in the Aguarico Community that was able to stop domestic violence.

One of the women's projects was to learn how to make clothes for the family. We had a classroom where we met, but there were no chairs, or tables. We needed a table to draw the patterns on.

The women were fast learners. The men cut four pieces from the trunk of a tree for table legs and used two planks (11 ½ inches wide x 6 feet long for the table top.) The table was rough, but they had a place to write and draw on and later, a place to cut the material...(see picture #14)

They wanted to make their own clothes but especially wanted to learn how to make their children's clothes. Some woman brought their old skirts and cut them up to practice on before they ventured with new material. Others learned how to knit infant socks, dresses, coats, etc and also learned how to crochet. Some of the ladies already knew how and volunteered to teach the young ones, but they had no material or thread.

We encouraged them to exercise by dancing. A social program was planned for the town which had a social hour featuring different folk dances. The women sewed their own costumes for the dance, and everyone was able to see what they had accomplished. It was another success to celebrate during a community gathering.

In the Aguarico Community, the women were able to accomplish much with the help of their husbands. The couples organized a dance to get the much needed funds for the materials. At the end of the year, we had an exhibition of all their works in their own centers. The women were proud of themselves seeing how much they had been able to accomplish and how they were able to help the economy of the family.

In the Santa Cruz Community, another group project was to grow rice together. We acquired the land, cleared it and planted the rice. We watched it grow and provided care for it. Because of the weather and the type of soil, it did not bear much fruit. The husbands, including the hesitant ones, were finally coming around as they observed the fruit of their wives' efforts. Later on, some groups started to make things to sell at the end of the year...(see picture #15)

With our reflection on the Word of God, we planned many themes according to the needs. We had general Bible study classes from the Old Testament, and it was so clear when we started the studies of the New Testament, conversion was coming in full.

They have found their secret, to know, love and serve God, in solidarity with the neighbors, in order to change society for the good of all. They were ready to walk with Jesus. They were ready to carry the cross. It was awesome to watch the wonders the Lord was doing in our land with His believers.

One of the special themes for the ladies was about: "Women in the Bible. We study one at a time and looked at the similarities to us in their conditions and solutions for problems.

As a Church, we were now moving towards a higher level of training. We invited two to four leaders from each group for training at the Mission Center. We would follow the same format. The following is an example of what they worked on at different conferences, assemblies, and or group meetings.

The goal

We were to discover and to accept the challenges presented to us as Christian women in the new evangelization.

Steps to get to those goals

• To analyze the present condition of the women in the area.

Each woman would tell her story; such as how she had to leave her place of birth to find a better way of life and found a totally different and unexpected reality. Some were ill because of loneliness with no neighbors and no one to talk to in addition; they lacked the basic necessities of life such as soap, sugar, clothes and shoes.

Others suffered in their relationships with their husbands. The fear the women experienced because of their surroundings was crippling them. Listening to each other gave them strength as they found they were not alone.

• How to value a woman's participation in the family and in the culture.

The women learned how to appreciate one another and how to value themselves. Not because of who they were married to but because God made them beautiful and precious in His eyes. One of the women's comments was,

"The most wonderful thing to me was finding out I am a part of God's plan from the beginning."

- *To study the reality of women in Ecuador and Latin America.*

Women began to see themselves in God's larger picture. This was definitely helpful to them. They listened to experiences of other groups at a national level which were having similar life experiences, in their struggles and victories. This knowledge gave them strength.

- *To deepen their understanding of the characteristics of the New Evangelization.*

We looked at a godly life from the view point of the poor, the suffering, and the downtrodden. How did Jesus treat them during his life on earth? We looked at the kind of life and the struggles Jesus had to go through. We were able to see both the humanity and the divinity of Jesus.

- *To discover the challenges in the future.*

Reflecting on the day-to-day situations, they discovered their own abilities to cope and change as the demands came in their families and in the community. We needed to stop, reflect, and go on; we must trust in the greater plan from God and surrender to him.

- *To take concrete responsibility as Christian women individually and as a Church.*

When a woman wanted to attend one of the training weekends, this created other demands. If her children came with her; she needed to make sure her teenagers or children attended the meetings dedicated to them, allowing them to study and grow spiritually also. Those leaders who planned to go to the training without their children needed someone to care for the family while they were gone. How to get the women released from their duties at home was a challenge. In the small groups, each leader presented her desire to attend and her difficulties in doing so.

The solution

In the case of a woman having to go for a whole weekend, they discovered the solution. The women who stayed home would become part of the project. One woman would volunteer to have the children for the weekend. Another woman volunteered to have the meals ready for the men that were working in the fields. Another would take the responsibility of feeding the animals.

In the beginning, it was very difficult to imagine this solution, but as the group grew in love, wisdom and understanding of the Word of God, solidarity became easier. It became a matter of course that the ones who could not go would take care of the family left behind.

This modeled a way of dealing with other community needs. It was awesome to see how God's Word was working in each one of them. At the beginning, if the husband did not attend the meetings, it was very difficult for him to understand and to join in the life of loving like God wanted them. Some men forbid their wives to attend the meetings for fear of losing control of them and one even said, "She is going to know more than me and will not obey me." After a while, as he experienced the benefits. He saw the members working hard for the whole community.

He would not only allow the wife to attend the meetings but also helped with chores and children at home. Salvation was in each home; the happiness and understanding of one another, among neighbors, friends, and relationships between couples were improving.

The National Congress for Woman

This Congress was another learning experience for me. It was amazing to see the women's enthusiasm and their desire to be part of the larger picture. They expressed how they felt through me. I took a report of what was going on in *"The Woman's department of the Sucumbíos Church."* The women were surely present in spirit in all my presentations. We all felt the spirit of unity and the power that comes from that. We were building a new world, the New Creation that was promised by our Savior Jesus Christ. The women were learning little by little how to lead a group. My goal was that they would be able to organize a conference and they would run it themselves.

Most of the women's educational backgrounds were through grade school only, and some did not know how to read and write. However, they overcame all the difficulties. They involved their teenagers to help in the parts that needed reading and writing on the chalkboard. Their creativity in finding solutions was encouraging to me and them. This was empowering *"teaching them how to fish, not just giving them a fish."*

Many of the male and female roles had to be dealt with. We reflected on mothers, aunts, sisters, and friends, stereotypes that were passed on from generation to generation. How to change these traditions and amend these stereotypes in a way pleasing to God would be a challenge.

We read the Bible and meditated on what kind of person Mary, the Mother of Jesus, was in order to be able to do what she did. Young as she was, she went to help her older cousin.

It took a very brave strong woman to take that trip as Mary did in her condition.

While we were studying each woman of the primitive church, there were some women in the community who gave testimonies of their own experiences to encourage one another. Little by little, they were discovering their own and each other's strengths and God given gifts. The women came to their own conclusion about the role God wanted for them. To be a part of Gods plan loving and living as a Christian sharing the good news that Jesus died to forgive our sins and to give us eternal life.

At the different conferences, we all came out enriched and we learned from each other how to be a better person and a better Christian.

During the presentation of their own skits, according to the theme, their personal reality would come across and along with it, the solution. Whatever spiritual gift each one had, it was as if it was unwrapped and shared with the rest of the group.

Each leader went back home to the group to which she belonged. She shared what she had learned as she continued growing step by step not only as an individual but along with the group.

Like a pebble makes a circle in the water, the bigger the pebble the bigger the circle. In the same way, each one was starting to understand that she had an influence in the family, among friends in the church and in society.

Visit to the community of Santa Barbara/El Playon

Four of us went to visit a community in the highlands (La sierra.) to work with them for one week, three of us from the group COIM, and one companion. We were not prepared for the trip. We were told it was about a three hour walk after the car left us.

It took us all day long. We walked with our back packs and drank whatever water we found by the road. I had some candy and every hour I would give each one a piece of candy to maintain their energy. About three o'clock in the afternoon, we went by a sugar cane plantation. Our companion went in; he (a young man from the city) pulled up cane with his bare hands, and we were able to rest for a while and enjoy the sugar cane. It had sweet water in the middle pulp after you peeled the stalk off. We still had no idea how much farther we needed to walk.

Finally, about five in the afternoon, we arrived at a corn field. We started to build a fire to cook some corn. As we were trying to get the fire started, we saw a person walking on the road. We asked "How far are we from the mission center?" He answered, "Just a little more. Walk around the bend and you can see it." The energy came back to us, all of a sudden and we all stood up, put out the fire and ran to see if it was true.

Down in the valley, the town was peacefully and beautifully laid out. It was an awesome scene and spectacular to us. The town was alive with children. As soon as they saw us, they started running to meet us. We arrived at the mission center. No one was prepared for our coming because the radio had not been working, and there was no way to inform them of our visit.

We were very cold and hungry. Once again we went to find something to eat in the garden. We found some sweet tomatoes that were not ripe, but we ate them anyway. The cook took a long time to start the fire. Then we had soup to warm us up. We were shivering and sitting as close to the fire as possible to warm up.

There was very little fire wood which was used for cooking only. The caretakers of the mission were very apologetic for the lack of knowledge about our arrival and the lack of food in store to cook much of anything. We were very grateful for whatever she was able to come up with.

The night came soon, and without electricity, we sparingly used the small pieces of candle for light. The three of us women huddled in one bed to be able to warm up, which took a long time, while our companion went with the couple. We prayed thanking God for all His blessings and asking for our needs to be met as we had to be there for the whole week.

We made a schedule of activities for the time we were going to spend there. First priority was to start visiting two or three families in their homes. It was an old town with adobe houses and with not much firewood close by. All the trees had been chopped down. Each family sparingly used the wood only for cooking. We were invited to the kitchen and offered a cup of coffee with a piece of bread.

We invited them to the women's group meeting and the Christian Community meeting. Everyone welcomed us into their homes so happily; it made us feel good.

The ladies came to the meeting and reported what had been going on including their needs, successes, and failures. They had a co-op where they grew "cuyes" (a small rabbit like animal with short ears) whose white meat is very delicious to eat. We went to see how they took care of the animals and what was going on. They were well organized and had many projects. Some projects had been given up because they did not work out, and some new projects were about to be started. They had classes on sewing and crocheting and were working on the items they could afford to make.

The community meeting was very interesting as they told amazing stories of the old times when the place was full of trees and wild animals. The people told of the pilgrims who started the town. They remembered their parents and grandparents and talked about how the first missionaries had come to them, with the Word of God.

They talked about how now the new Community leaders were helping to reflect on the Word of God and working together in solidarity. Once again, we were being evangelized by these people and grateful for the opportunity to be with them. We met many people, poor and rich, with great hearts.

When the week was over and it was time to go back, we had no physical companion to walk with us. We had God, his Angels and the three of us women to walk in the wilderness all day. The lady fixed us some food, to take with us for the trip. We thanked her and all of those who came around to say good bye and wished us well. After a long day, we arrived at the paved road. The sun was going down and we needed to hitch a ride. We prayed it would come soon but we had to wait awhile.

Safe from a man called Satan

It was already dark when a jeep stopped and picked us up. When we introduced ourselves, the driver said, "If I had known you were missionaries, I would have not picked you up.

I just thought you were three beautiful young ladies with

a guitar; I had a desire to have a good time tonight. My name is Satan; I am from Saint Gabriel town and was on my way home. I am a business man who makes living selling potatoes." The other passenger with him smiled very strangely and said his name was Jose.

Praying to God for the right words, I told him that "My dad was born in that town, and we still have some family there. I started talking very fast. Then he became interested about which family I came from. (The Jimenez family) I said. His response was that he knew them, what they did, and where they lived he sounded disappointed.

After some silence, he asked, "Why are you missionaries?" For him this type of life did not make sense at all. He definitely was not a believer. How could he understand? This was our chance, so I told him about God. "God is a God of love and cares for all of us. Right now he is taking care of us even through him by providing a ride for us." I reminded him that "Jesus died for him also." We had a good discussion about angels, good and bad.

I felt the seed was falling on good ground. He must have been searching because the tone in the conversation changed and we became friends after riding a couple of very long hours to the city.

The three of us in the back seat were holding hands tightly and praying the whole time. We were at the mercy of these men in an unknown place. We trusted in God's protection, and were kept safe. They took us to the bus station, plus he gave us a bag of one hundred pounds of potatoes, which he was carrying on top of the jeep.

It was another miracle in our lives. God was at work all the time. Later when we remembered that experience, we realized God wanted that man to hear about Him.

Chapter 11

At Last, Our Very Own Home

"That they all may be one, as you Father; you are in me and I in You. That they also may be one in us, that the world may believe that you sent me."

John 17: 21 (TNAB)

Saint Vincent was a Christian-based community named after the great saint of the poor in the Catholic Church. This community is located northeast of Quito, the capitol of Ecuador. The people here were mostly newcomers from the *Loja Province* a city which had the longest drought on record, causing many people and most living things to die. According to the recollections of some who had lived there, the government's solution was to offer fifty acres of jungle land to each family who was willing to move there and cultivate it. A plane had flown over the drought area dropping pamphlets to offer new land, where there was water.

Many families responded and moved with just their bare necessities, leaving a hostile parched land behind, for a land of plenty. It was a different world for them. They saw lush green trees and all kinds of tropical vegetation, plus wild exotic animals that inhabited and thrived in the jungle.

The wild animals and abundant water were a challenge for them in the beginning. Many times I saw where garbage that had been thrown out, sprouting seeds taking root where they had landed. The newcomers needed to learn how to deal with all the changes, especially the water. They bathed near the river shore or creek by using a small cup to pour the water over their heads. It was fun for me to teach the children and women how to be friends with the water by bathing and swimming. The way they built their homes was very practical; high above the ground, to protect them from the night animals and from flooding when tropical rains came. Missionaries had been visiting this community for some time.

The people were organized enough to have their own leaders, who knew the process of building a Christian Community. This was where we bought a piece of land for the new "COIM" group for the Sucumbíos Church.

With money from friends in the USA, one of them was Reverend Nathe, we kept in contact. I wrote to him about the mission where I was and what I was doing and the terrible situation people lived in. He sent five hundred dollars once a year to help with the project of educating and evangelizing. His generosity was such a wonderful blessing to the mission. We were able to purchase five acres of land which included two acres of coffee bean plants and one acre of bananas ready to be harvested.

First we started building the house for the women so that we would be able to move in as soon as possible. After that, the goal was to build a house for men and a house for couples. They would be constructed only as funds came in.

The people were very friendly. They found out through word of mouth that the missionaries would be coming to live among them. Everyone expressed joy and delight about the news. The community leaders gathered everyone together to welcome us and give us a hand in getting settled quickly.

We knew most of the people. Our group was under a different name than before so we had to explain why we had changed our name, and the new way things would be carried out. We explained that COIM's objectives were to evangelize and serve communities through the Church by living out our

Christian lives in practical ways. The Church must always present the gospel of Jesus Christ if it wants to maintain its freshness and strength.

We would help the people understand this great dream and project of Monsignor Gonzalo, who had started the group with me for the local church. The group would no longer be exclusively women. There would also be men and couples who would live as the first Christians had lived communally, sharing the goods and working together as one big family, the Church.

Eventually, we built a chicken house where wild animals would not be able to get to the chickens. Our idea was to have eggs and chicken to eat and sell. This would add to our income from the coffee beans and bananas...(see picture #16)

We were very united with those around us and felt we were accomplishing our objective to live simply as they lived. It was from here we would evangelize and serve the people of the area.

The house was finally completed! We moved from 10 of August (*La Diez de Agosto*) *Community* into our new home that had two bedrooms and an open space for the kitchen, living room and chapel. There were plenty of bushes to conceal us when nature called. A road was about 300 feet from our house. A small creek ran through our land adding a special beauty.

Our neighbors

Directly across the road lived a family with for children, pigs, chickens and two big dogs. They were coffee producers. At the side of their house was a large cement slab that looked like a parking lot. It was a little higher in the middle so that water would run down on both sides. It was used for drying coffee beans before taking them to market in Lago Agrio. Coffee beans brought straight from the trees sold for a lower price than beans, which had been dried first.

The workers harvesting the coffee beans would put them on the cement slab and then the lady of the house would spread them out letting the heat of the sun dry them.

One afternoon, I saw a storm coming and realized the neighbor lady was trying to gather all the coffee beans by herself to keep the rain off of them or they would be ruined. I ran over to help. She was grateful because there was no one else at home. We hurried! I had never pushed coffee beans in my life and I did not realize how heavy they were! We pushed the coffee beans to the center of the slab to make a long ridge near the highest spot. I gave it all I had and as the first raindrops fell, we were able to cover the beans with a big blue plastic tarp.

I went back home exhausted with a side ache, a headache, and muscle aches, that lasted a long time. It was the last time I volunteered to help her gather the coffee beans. When the other Sisters came back that night, I told them about it and they responded, "You should not have done that. It was too hard for you and your health is not good."

But this was the way every farmer and his wife work. The men gather and do the most strenuous work. The woman and children work very hard also, but they are used to it.

I felt bad for the women. They had to take care of their children, the animals and the house. They also helped with the business. These pioneer women are very strong and have learned to take one day at a time, in this simple but difficult life. It amounts to survival. I admired them so much and kept learning from them.

The neighbors house on fire

Next to our land was a new family with children, who had a very simple house made of bamboo and palm. One night while we were eating, our dog kept barking until one of the sisters went out to see why and called out in alarm, "The neighbor's house is burning!" We ran with buckets of water to help. Just in time we brought the children out.

The oldest daughter had thrown out a box of dirty clothes but it was too late to save anything else.

The flames were shooting up to the sky, lighting the whole area. Things were exploding once in a while, until there was only smoke and quietness. In fifteen minutes the house was gone. We were in shock!

The gathering neighbors knew that the parents of the children had gone to visit relatives. Someone volunteered to go to let them know about their home. We brought the children into our home and thanked God their lives had been saved. We took care of the burns first; then we drank some tea to calm our nerves and started trying to figure out how we were going to manage with the children before the parents came back. Our plans for the next day had to be postponed. We gathered all the bedding we could spare and made a bed for them on the floor.

The next day, we looked for clothes they could wear. Our blouses were big enough to use as long dresses for the girls. The boy had to wear what he had on the day before. I wanted them to continue their routine as much as possible. That meant the three older ones would go to school with their friends and be with the teacher who knew them.

We fed them and sent them off to school which wasn't too far. They were assured they had a place to come back to and that their parents were on their way. Now, only the two-year-old needed to be cared for.

The oldest girl told us what had caused the fire. She was studying for her fifth grade test and fell asleep. Her head dropped down, which hit the lamp (*Chimbuso*) with diesel fuel in it, catching the bamboo wall on fire. She awoke when her clothes were ablaze and her arm was burned. She woke up her brothers and sisters and threw out the first thing she found, which was a box of dirty clothes. The explosions were caused by her father's guns, gun powder and some paint he had started buying for the house he planned to build in the future.

That day we focused on giving thanks to God for sparing the children's lives. It was a great blessing that the children had suffered only minor wounds. We could care for these wounds with herbs. The emotional and spiritual wounds would take more time.

The parents finally arrived in the late afternoon. The women's group started organizing to help them.

As is customary, in Ecuador, a team carried a flag from house to house to ask for help. Everyone gave as much as they could, which was very little. The group I led headed for the city to ask the big companies for help; and immediately received some material to build a small cement house with a tin roof. The family's great loss affected us all, in different ways. The unity and purpose of the group, at this time of need showed a true Christian attitude.

We were grateful for our dog that had warned us, enabling us to save the children. After my youngest brother Virgilio heard we had lost all of our chickens at the last place we lived. He gave us a beautiful German shepherd; we called "*Paloma.*" She was a good watch dog and people would ask for her puppies, but every time she had some they would die.

Some months later, we received a Saint Bernard from my brother Ricardo. We called her "Osa." She was a blessing in many ways, not only taking care of us by barking to let us know when people were coming.

She regularly gave us big, beautiful, healthy puppies. We loved her. She was a very gentle animal and a good mother.

The neighbors and people around the area liked Osa and wanted her puppies but I did not sell them. I said I would exchange a puppy for a chicken. One time she gave us ten puppies, which meant ten chickens. That is how we got started raising chickens again, but not before we built them a safe chicken coop with a cement floor, screened-in walls and a tin roof.

The family on the other side of our land consisted of a child and a young woman with a very jealous husband. She would come and talk to me when her husband was not home. She had some serious emotional and mental problems. He would not let her join the women's group. It became harder to help her. Then one day he realized her problems were too big for him. He could not help her.

That is when they joined the Christian Community and made Jesus the center of their lives.

It sure makes a big difference when someone finds out what God wants, of each of us and commits his life to Jesus our Savior. As the family started to attend the meetings, it was wonderful to see changes in their actions.

The generosity of my family at the mission

My birth family loved me so much and always supported and helped me in any way they could to fulfill my dreams. Although they may not have agreed on the choices I had made for my life. My brothers thought it was a hard way to live but they were willing to help. Some of my family wanted to enjoy the summer away from the city they lived in. Although they knew we had no electricity or running water they still wanted to visit and work.

Ricardo is a very dear brother to me. He chose to stay home and work with my dad while the rest of us went to college. He found a good wife, Guadalupe and they have three children at that time, Omar (12), Richard (11), and Santiago (3), who loved to play with the our dog Osa.

Celso, my next younger brother and his wife Julia who are both teachers in Quito also came to help. They brought their two little girls Katita,(5) and Doris, (3). The two couples with their children stayed in one room and the rest of us in the other. Julia and the girls had a hard time with mosquito bites which would swell up and itch where their skin wasn't covered. You couldn't keep them from scratching. They declared the mosquitoes as their worst enemy. I was sorry we did not have mosquito nets for anyone.

My brothers had learned carpentry from our dad, when they were young. They worked from sun up to sun down. We used our *"chimbusos"* for light when it was getting dark. Their first project was to build a wooden outhouse with a wooden toilet seat so we wouldn't have to squat any more. They made a door that would not fly open with the wind and a roof made of palm leaves to protect us from the rain.

The next thing we needed was a kitchen dining room combination. It would be a separate building close to the house which would keep the smoke from getting inside the bedrooms.

Then we happily moved the cooking utensils out of the house, it gave us more sleeping accommodations. For at least one of the two weeks, the families were less cramped.

The next project (a precious jewel to us) was the beautiful hexagon chapel by the creek about ninety feet from the house. The floors were laid piece by piece. They were mahogany. Ricardo designed the floor to look like the table of the "Last Supper." The roof was made of palm leaves. The big screen windows let the air in and we could see out while we prayed and contemplated God's creation without the mosquitoes.

My sisters-in-law, nieces and nephews helped by bring the wood to be cut and holding it. The ladies prepared meals for everyone and took refreshments to my brothers for a little break. Although my brothers never stopped; just for fun they did take a quick bath in the creek after work. In the afternoon the women and children could hardly wait to swimming to have fun. The creek was part of our land; so it was private and we didn't worry about having an audience.

My brothers were rightfully proud of their handiwork and we were so grateful! When the chapel was finished, we moved the things we used for praying out of the house and into the chapel. That made another space, in the room, for sleeping. We prayed as a group in the newly built chapel. It was such a blessing to bring our hearts together as we praised God.

The family of another sister came to visit and brought a colorful parrot that my niece Katita loved but was afraid to touch. My brother Celso remembers trying to teach her how to hold her finger out for the parrot to climb on. After two weeks of intensive work, it was hard for me to say goodbye to my family. However, they had to take care of their own needs at home. Though much work remained to be done, with their help, we were much more comfortable. With the extra room and our basic needs met, we felt we could start a routine and get organized.

A Sister from the Teresita's Community came to live with us to help in the Spirituality of St. Teresa of Avila, the Carmelite.

She was very practical and even helped us make some benches to seat the visitors. She was used to her own room and now we had one because my brothers had left...(see picture #17)

The Sister told stories of her life in her religious community and why she stayed there. It was good to have a different Sister talking about how religious life is for women. The young Sisters were a good audience, soaking in the information. She was an encouragement to me. She expressed her admiration at what I was doing and how it was God's will for me. She stayed with us for two weeks.

God moves the Governor

One day, it came to our attention that the big landlords of the area were planning to build a center for prostitution and entertainment called A.B.C. It was to be built at the crossing of our road and the main road to Quito. The foundations for it were already laid. The school was close by so we understood the moral and physical danger it presented. We got together with the leaders and people of the community to discuss this problem.

We prayed and asked God for guidance. We had already gone to the local authority but our request fell on deaf ears. We decided to go to the Governor and ask him to stop that building. Fifteen people were chosen to go. Some would stay home to take care of the children, animals, and feed the men when they came back from work. Those who could not do that would help pay the bus tickets of those going. It was quite amazing how all the whole community was involved.

We took the bus in the evening and by early morning we arrived at Tena the location of the Governor's office. We washed up as much as we could, ate breakfast and then went over the plans of what we were going to do. We didn't want the authorities to know because we would be stopped before we could see the Governor. It "just happened" that his secretary was one of my college classmates, so I was given the first appointment in the morning when the Governor arrived.

We planned that only three of us would be obviously waiting to see him. Not wanting to call attention to ourselves as a group, we would scatter around in the park in front of the building. These would be waiting alone or in twos. When the appointed person gave a whistle, everyone would run to get past the door before the guard could shut it. The waiting was nerve-racking until the Governor came and we followed him in.

He smiled and said, "How can I help you?"

We explained our problem and he answered, "If the Commissioner there cannot do anything to stop the building of the entertainment center, I can't go above him."

We all sat down on the floor as one person and responded, "We will stay here until you do, because you do have the authority, and we know you can stop it." He became impatient and nervous. The room was getting hot and he started perspiring.

He looked at the guard, and said, "I can ask him to take you out or call for more help."

We responded, "There are too many of us.

You don't want a riot in your office do you? We want peace and safety for our community. It is too far from any police to call for help. There are many deaths in the cities near areas where there is prostitution and the police can't do much to stop that either. How would it be for us who are so isolated?" We had practiced what to say and each one of us knew when to speak.

He said, "What you are doing is illegal. It is like kidnapping and you can't do this. I have to continue working and I can't have you all here interrupting this way." He said he knew my father, and made a comment about it. Our group was at peace because we knew everyone was praying for the success of this undertaking, that God would intervene and find a way to soften the governor's heart. The governor made a couple of phone calls and said, "You can go now, the building will be stopped."

"Oh no!" we answered. "We need a written statement to show them. If we go back as we came, they will laugh at us. They will continue building and we will start burning it down. This will show them we mean business. We are saving our community."

He called the secretary and dictated a notice to stop the work immediately. We asked him to give us three copies. We needed one copy of the notice to take to the Commissioner, one to the owner of the business and one for us to keep. He smiled and said, "The secretary will wire the Commissioner from here."

We thanked him but we wanted to make sure it was done. We waited until we received the copies; we thanked him again and promised to pray for him. From under her poncho, one of the ladies brought out a parakeet and gave it to him. He laughed and thanked her and we cleared out of that very hot room.

We were overjoyed and laughing on our way back. We praised God for His intervention. The people saw how unity and faith does move mountains. This time the mountain was the Governor.

Construction of a building for the men

A building was constructed for the men on another portion of our land. Macario, Jose and Grivaldo moved in. Now when Monsignor came to stay, he had a place of his own.

Others candidates also used this new building. It was about ninety feet from the women's house. It was made of cement, wood and metal. Two bathrooms and a place to wash clothes were built beside the house. A big tank was placed on top of the building to collect water for the bathrooms and other needs.

The enemy in our midst

The dynamics changed when men were added to the group some positive, some negative. We decided, for example to build a front porch on the women's house. This would provide a place to meet and talk with visitors. One of the newcomers of the group had been out ministering in a neighboring community when the idea developed. He came back and saw the porch, he was furious! He demanded, "Who give permission to build this porch? It is not needed; we should have discussed it first!" It was a source of tension, and division for the group. Another new member agreed with him, and obviously there was dissention beginning within our group.

When the group was only women, we did not have a problem building anything that we saw necessary. One of the projects was a pier that protruded to the middle of the creek. We prayed there or just watched the fish swim around. On some afternoons, I played my guitar and we sang all kinds of songs. The pier provided a wonderful times of recreation and growing spiritually in different ways.

When Monsignor Gonzalo came to stay awhile with the group, he gave us clear spiritual goals. We evaluated how the pastoral work was going and each time the group relationships seemed harder and harder. It was difficult to take all the changes at once. Our spirituality and humanity was not strong enough to be able to overcome all the difficulties. There was power struggle within the group.

When new ones came into our group they came with new ideas that were foreign to those who had started the group. One of our men wrote what he perceived as part of the problem.

"In our search for unity, it is natural to have crisis. We seemed to have plenty. The causes are the many differences within our group such as our cultural backgrounds and being male and female. Some of us are more intellectually prepared, some spiritual, the academic levels are varied and our ways of life are very different. The goal is to come to a balance by sharing resources. Recognizing our strengths and weaknesses should be an incentive to help acknowledge mistakes, and ask forgiveness. If that is what is needed." [10]

This was amazing to us that this unlearned man could so easily see and speak to the problem. I truly believe that God had revealed this through him.

When we were first trying to consolidate ideas for the group, Monsignor Gonzalo said he wanted women who would "do the things women do to support the men." I suggested that men and women should be willing to do the same things, although I felt men would find it difficult to do "women's work" because of their cultural background. Much later he changes that idea.

A power struggle was occurring. Another example was that I wanted the young Sisters to have the opportunity to see other places. With money my friends had sent from the United States.

We four girls had traveled a couple of times when our group was only women. To me, it was a worthwhile expense. But that had to stop because, according to one member specifically. "The poor farmers do not have that opportunity." Clearly, "He wanted to take over the lead."[11] It was clearly gender discrimination. Some considered it a struggle between the nationals versus the foreigners, which cast a dark shadow upon us.

The men and women were used to being treated differently. I was training the sisters that we were both, male and female, made in God's image. This group was formed with the idea of accomplishing God's work in a diverse way; where everyone was to share and share alike whether you were a man or woman. The younger men accepted this more easily.

Monsignor's humble spirit, a light for all to see.

I saw Monsignor Gonzalo's humility when he was the first to take a broom to sweep the floor and then helped clear the table. This picture was hard for the young women to see. They were so use to being the "servants" to the men. They wanted to take the broom away from him.

He also worked in the vegetable garden with us, or cook if necessary. Their comments were, "He is a Bishop and according to custom, he should not be doing that type of work.".(See picture #18)

We had previously discussed with the Bishop about the women's education. Somehow in the process and with his illness it had been put aside. He was not present during the fast development and growth of the group. I have his words in my notes: "Yes, the sisters will be allowed to study but do not think you are going to send them to Harvard in the United States." We had a good laugh. I wanted to make sure everyone would have the opportunity to study and get their certificates.

We held classes for everyone at the Center. Various subjects were taught by Missionary teachers from Pacifico Zambrano College. I also wanted our members to have the opportunity to go to a public school or college to earn a diploma. We were able to send Mary to the Napo College of Lago Agrio. Noemi was sent for a course in Central America, and Macario went to Panama.

Isabel was already a teacher but I thought and expressed, "What about the rest of the young sisters; Gladys, Elida, Inez, Mery the Shuar?" They should also be given the opportunity if they desired to study.

COIM was a great idea, but as time went by it became more difficult to be of one heart. My health was declining rapidly. We were all giving as much as we could to God. We needed development for the people in many areas especially the ones who had the least. As a woman, I felt badly for the women of our community. The men had so many more opportunities in life. Changes to this age old tradition came so very slowly.

Harvesting coffee beans

One of our continual activities was to weed the field to make sure the coffee bean plants would be healthy and produce a good harvest. Harvesting coffee beans was a new experience for me. Everyone had a plastic bucket hanging from their neck. With both hands you hold the top of the branch and drag down the coffee beans to the container. The sisters and the young men showed me how to do it. They did it so easily.

When I tried it turned out to be more of an exercise of my arms than any coffee beans going in the container. As soon as I took hold of the branch, dozens of ants would rapidly crawl onto my fingers and arms and run up to my neck. I would have to shake them off. It was just about impossible to get anything done since the ants are faster than lightening and their bites are painful.

One day I proposed to the team that I would stay home during this activity. I was not much help. By the time it took them to gather sixteen buckets to get one hundred pounds I had verily gathered one bucket full. My thinking was there was much I could do at home while they were harvesting.

Their unanimous response to that suggestion was very rewarding. Almost in chorus they said, "No! You can't stay home! We need you. Who is going to make us sing while we are harvesting? Who is going to make us scream silly things across the field just to know we are not alone in the field? We have done this before, but it was never so much fun. You brought that to us and we don't want to miss it."

They assured me that, after awhile I would not even notice the ants were crawling on me. I said, "I will welcome that time and bless the ants." I felt appreciated and it was very fulfilling.

Rescuing 3 sexually abused girls

In the late afternoon, a mother brought her daughter to us. The mother was crying and begged me not to go to the authorities because her husband would kill her, and she had other children to look after.

That night our dog started barking. We woke up hearing a man's voice saying, "Maria Luisa, you'd better come out. I have a bullet with your name on it! You cannot take my daughter away. I know you have her here."

We were very frightened! We could hear him coming closer and closer. Everyone could tell by his slurred speech that he was drunk. Paloma, our dog could not stop him. The man was not afraid of her and hit her. We heard her yelp and run under the house. The men of our group were at the Mission Center in Aguarico for a week-long seminar.

We piled all the things we could find against the door to block it. At the same time, Mary and Elida ran out the back door to ask for help from the closest neighbor, the one we had helped with their burning home. It was dark and a soft rain was falling so they put their boots on and hurried out.

I prayed to God, "It is your daughter. Help us to protect her. Protect us all." Our other neighbor shot into the air a couple of times but nothing was stopping this man. My name kept being called. I went into the room to check on the girl and she was peacefully asleep. I could not believe it, but I thanked God for that.

Finally, we heard another man's calm voice calling him by name to stop. When the sisters came back they told us that our neighbor was a relative of the drunken man. As we heard the girl's father start to come up the steps, his cousin ran to get hold of him. He was talking smoothly and calming him down, letting him know what would happen if he did shoot me. They sat on the front steps and over and over he said, "I want to kill Maria Luisa. She is taking my daughter away."

I was shaking but feeling better because his cousin was there. He took the rifle away from the girl's father; we heard the whole conversation. At dawn he finally convinced the drunken man to stop his threats and took him home.

As soon as the sun came up, I went to Aguarico and took the girl to a Brother. He would drive her to Lumbaqui where other missionaries would get her on the bus where Ruben was waiting with the other two girls. Three girls in all had been brought to me because of sexual abuse. I worked with The Good Shepherd Sisters in Quito who took care of girls in trouble. We were trying to keep the situation quiet, as many lives depended on it. We worked out a plan to get the girls to Quito, but not all at the same time or from the same area. One of the leaders was to deliver the girls to the Good Shepherd Sisters. He was to gather them from three different places and the last girl was to be waiting for him at the bus station in Lumbaqui.

One girl vanished

According to Macario's notes, they were in Aguarico at the Conference when they received a message for me from Ruben. They came to tell me Ruben had only taken two girls in Quito. The girl we had sent to Lumbaqui was not at the bus station. I called a women's meeting, and one of the ladies, volunteered to go with me to Lumbaqui. On the way she told me her sad story; why she really wanted to help this girl. She had suffered the same thing and had a limp because of sexual abuse when she was five. She said, "I'll do whatever is necessary to help you find her."

We drove to Lumbaqui but the missionary team knew nothing. I discovered the Brother had left the girl at the convent. The Sisters were gone at that time and never saw her. We went from house to house asking if they had seen a girl. We gave her description but it was not until a couple of hours of walking and asking had passed, that the owner of one of the shops said he saw her standing under a palm tree for a while, until a gas truck came by and she climbed on.

Macario and Jose went to the girl's family to let them know what had happened. Macario, stayed outside to be back up help, if necessary, while Jose went in to tell them their daughter was lost. The mother said, "She may have gone to her aunt's house." The next day, two other ladies and I went to the aunt's house and yes the girl was there. We asked what happened.

The girl said, "No one answered the door at the convent and I did not know anyone. I waited then decided to go to my aunt. I got on the truck and went."

The aunt said, "I did not believe my brother would do such horrible things and thought she was lying. I took her to the Doctor and found it was true. I am so ashamed of him. I thank God for you, Sister Maria Luisa. How can I pay you?"

I assured her there was no need for that. The girl's security was what I was interested in. I felt better. It was good that the aunt stood up for the girl. I talked to both of them separately and then together.

The aunt wanted to adopt her and not allow her brother near her. The girl wanted to stay with her.

It took ten days for all the arrangements to be finalized. This resolved situation allowed room for another girl at the Good Shepherd Sisters. I never saw that man or the mother of the girl again. I heard later they had moved. The man's cousin expressed his shame and embarrassment.

Some young men and women had been part of the journey. They joined us, stayed awhile and left, but life goes on. We were all a part of God's plan. The body of Christ was alive and expressing itself in many ways. Our ministry was being fruitful, because of this many came to know and love God.

Chapter 12

Walking with the Poor

*"Show me your way, O Lord,
lead me on a level path because of my enemies
Do not abandon me to the will of my foes;
Wait for the Lord, take courage;
Be stouthearted, wait for the Lord.*

Psalm 27: 11-12 (TNAB)

Even though the testing did not stop, we continued learning our lessons and giving thanks to God for His care and protection. During these hard times, the group continued to make this home as beautiful as possible; making it a place of prayer, joy, and living as good Christians should. "Look at them how they love one another." We worked on two gardens at the same time. On one side, in front of the women's house, was the medicinal herb garden. Many times, when people came for help, we were able to offer a cup of herb tea which helped fill their need. Taking a lesson from what they had seen in our home, they started to follow our example in their homes. We began to exchange herbs and explain the uses of each one.

In front of the chapel was the flower garden. When we didn't have time to cut the flowers and put them in vases inside the chapel, we just had to look out the windows to enjoy Gods creation. There was a small pier on the creek that ran on the side of the chapel. The view of the water, flowers, and trees was just gorgeous. We loved it and were proud we had made our home and the surroundings just as we liked. We wanted the inner beauty to come out too. We were sure we would see and experience the goodness of the Lord right here and now.

Each day we faced challenges and some contradictions with one another because we were so different in the way we thought and how we did things. This caused difficulties and was something we never anticipated. The enemy was pounding on us from all sides through constant spiritual battles Monsignor Gonzalo's vision and dream seemed impossible.

My health was deteriorating more and more. I found that the group had gone to Monsignor Gonzalo and asked him to assign me to communities closer to the Mission center.

They saw how my energy was being drained. The different communities were too far away and demanded sacrifices; I didn't have strength to complete.

A celebration of a child's death

We received a request to come to a home where a child had died. When the two of us arrived, we saw an unexpected picture. On the patio the family had placed a table as an altar by one of the walls of the house. On and around it were all kinds of flowers from the garden and the jungle. It was beautiful. Many lighted candles were around the altar and in the center was a throne. It was a chair beautifully decorated with white flowers and on that small throne sat the dead child dressed in white, with a crown of white flowers on her head.

The mother was standing by the kitchen door in a state of numbness. Her face showed the utter sadness which was coming from within her. It was very understandable; there was not much to say. I could only hug her and hold her. Then I realized there was music and children were dancing in front of the altar.

I may have looked surprised because someone explained to me. "This is the way we celebrate, as in heaven, where the child is pure and is with God so we need to rejoice! She will never suffer again and go through troubles like we do here. She is with the angels and is happy now, so we dance."

The children seemed to have done this before and were happily dancing to the very joyful music that was typical for them. I love to dance but could not get myself to join in, as I had never before been in a celebration of death like this. I stayed with the mother. How long we were there, I don't recall but we were there in love and support. It did not take long for the men to build a coffin for the child.

Early the next morning, we returned to their home and followed the procession with the child's coffin to the cemetery. It was carried on the shoulders of four older children who were rotated after a short distance. We mostly sang songs of joy and praise on the way.

At the cemetery, the priest blessed the place where the child was laid to rest.

Everyone threw in a handful of dirt. We all prayed and sang and returned to the house to eat whatever the family had to offer. We sisters brought some food from our home to share as we knew there would be a lot of people.

I was listening to the ladies as they talked to the mother trying to console her. "You are young, there will be more children coming." And, "Now you have more time to take care of the rest of the children." For all the good will and consoling thoughts, she just silently cried.

We listened to the mother tell about how the child died. Her stomach was so big and all the teas she gave didn't stop the pain. She quit eating so the mother took her to Lago Agrio, where the doctor said the child was suffering from malnutrition, dehydration and was full of amoebas. He asked if the mother boiled the drinking water. She responded, "How could I, if I can barely get wood for cooking meals." The other ladies nodded their heads in agreement. I saw more and more how great the need was for basic hygiene and health education.

It was the theme we would talk about at the next women's meeting. We would ask a nurse from Lago Agrio to come and give a course on the importance of hygiene for the whole community and how to take care of the children's health.

A native Shuar joins COIM

Mery Sadia, one of our treasures for COIM, came to us in 1983. She was a young teenager from the Shuar tribe with only a grade school education who spoke Spanish and Shuar. She was from a community where their ancestors were great warriors and we called the "Shrinking heads." There is a legend that the heads of the warriors who lost the war were taken, to be boiled in a special mixture of herbs which would shrink the heads to the size of a fist. (Now, tourist love to buy plastic heads as souvenirs.) I wondered about Mary becoming part of our group. I did not speak Shuar and her Spanish wasn't very fluent.

The worst worry for me was the different culture and not being able to help her understand the concept of religious life as we were planning it. I did not want her to experience the pain I had gone through. I wanted to protect her.

This experience with her brought back memories of me when I had moved to the U.S.A. where the culture and language were different. How at times I felt out of place and I didn't understand what was going on. My ideas of what religious life experiences were different. But again, God was always there to intervene and help us. *"Look at the birds of the air, the flowers in the fields,"* I had to remind myself to trust God and surrender to Him.

I had no idea how Mary Sadia felt about family separation, which had been an issue for me. She was bright, good tempered and with her shyness and silence would let us know when she did not agree about something. She loved the time we spent working the land. That was her turf. She would laugh so freely at me and said, "That is not the way!" Then she'd proceed to show me how to do the job right, whether it was in the garden or in the field. She had a beautiful spirit and was a hard worker. I loved her very much.

One day, when it was time for community activities, we could not find her. We went looking, but where do you look to find her? In a field where she is most at home? After a couple of long hours we found her sitting by the creek close to the far end of our property. She may have heard us, but did not move or acknowledge it. She was sitting still with the most beautiful smile on her face and looked perfectly peaceful and contented. I thought "This is prayer."

When I asked her, "Mary why did you leave without letting anyone know where you would be? We have been worried you could have been hurt." Her facial expression changed immediately and she said; "You should know I'd be watching the fish." That explanation lost me, but I was happy we had found her. I replied, "The next time you feel like watching the fish, just let us know so we won't be concerned about you."

At times, the other sisters would be impatient with her. They told me, "When you are not present to tell her what to do, she doesn't want to obey." She was still a child that needed to be coached by an authority at all times.

The incident we had experienced was long past and I had forgotten about it when again, Mery was nowhere to be found. We went looking in all directions. First, to the place where we had found her before, but no, she was not there. Suddenly we heard a noise and went out to see what it was. She was sitting on top of the roof of the house by the water tank. It was the highest place she could find; to see the sky.

I decided to mention this to Monsignor Gonzalo and let her go home. She did not feel like she was a part of the group, and her way of life was very different from ours. When we talked to her about possibility of letting her go back home, her face lit up but she didn't say a word. We learned it had been her parent's idea for her join the group, more so than hers.

We talked to them and they came to take her home. She looked so happy and almost bounced as she went to her parents, brothers and sisters. This was not her type of life but I was sure she would be a good example of a growing Christian to the rest of the girls her age among her people. Maybe in the future there will be a specific group from and for her own tribe.

The Death of Our Prized dog, Paloma

Paloma was our dear German shepherd dog; who had been with us for a while now. She was given to us by my brother Virgilio to protect our house, chickens and belongings. She had become a wonderful guard dog. From the day the drunken man beat her so badly, she changed her happy personality. Later, when she didn't show up for her meal, we went looking for her. We called her and she didn't come.

After a long search, we found her under water in the creek, standing and almost smiling, but she was dead. Our young men came and took care of her body. I couldn't be a part, or even see how and where they buried her. It was a great loss and too much for me because we all had become attached to her. We grieved each in our own way. Paloma was a part of our family and gave us all a lot of joy and security.

Taking the law in our hands

Jose and Claudia a young couple came to talk to me. Claudia was pregnant and it was clear she had being crying.

Jose her husband, was nervous and said he didn't know how to start. I assured him, "Whatever it may be and God will help us and show us the way to be able to talk about it. We will be happy to help if we can.

He relaxed and started, "My wife had a terrible experience last week and I don't know how to help her." She hung her head and started crying a bit louder now. I held her hand and encourage him to go on. I couldn't imagine what the trouble could be. He said, "I don't know if I should kill them, or what. I am afraid." The young wife started crying some more. It was getting serious and the Holy Spirit came to my rescue. The questions started popping out of my mouth, leading them to tell me what it was because I could not get to the source of what their problem was. Then she started coughing, drying her tears and began to tell her horrendous experience.

She had been walking back from Lago Agrio and motioned for a ride to those in a truck hauling animal that was coming her way. There were two men in it that she knew and they stopped to pick her up.

She said they looked at each other and smiled as she climbed into the truck. They put her in between them.

As they were driving along where the road bends and the forest is thick, the driver said, "Now you have to pay your fare first before we take you home." They stopped the truck and made her come down from it. The owner of the truck grabbed her and forced her away from the road into the forest.

All her crying and begging and seeing she was very pregnant and hearing her expressed fear of harm to the baby who was due in two weeks did not stop this men. She had no more strength to fight. When he finished with her, he left her lying on the ground and called to the other man that it was his turn and that she was ready. The other man had his way with her also but this time she didn't beg and she didn't fight for she had no more energy. She just lay there. They carried her back to the truck because she could barely walk after the rape. They sat her by the window and literally pushed her out and dropped her by the entrance of the road to her house.

She couldn't tell her husband because she was afraid of what he would do. Of course, he saw her crying all the time and finally made her talk. Since they were part of the community and everyone knew them, they thought it would be best to come to us and ask if his thoughts about killing them were right. We talked about the consequences and the possibility that they would kill him first.

We prayed and asked God to help us. I was sure He would intervene, he always had. "God hears the cry of the poor." I asked the sisters to go to town and call a women's emergency meeting for the afternoon. We were going to solve this problem once and for all. I told Jose not to worry but to pray and wait. I made him promise not to do anything. We would help. The young couple left more peaceful than when they came in. I explained the facts; why we called the meeting and why we read these scriptures.

> *'Hear Oh Lord have mercy on me Lord,*
> *be my helper for I am in trouble;*
> *You change my mourning into dancing;*
> *You took off my sackcloth and clothed me with gladness. With my whole being I sing endless praises to you. Oh Lord my God, Forever I will give you thanks.*
>
> Psalm 30: 11-12 (TNAB)

We reflected on these verses and asked the Lord with all of our hearts to guide us, deliver us, and help us. We needed to trust God.

I was not able to hold back my outrage about the situation. "How can anyone be so calloused as to do this to a pregnant woman?" Then I expressed my fears for the young sisters I was responsible for and said, "If these evil men are not stopped, we are all in danger!" To my surprise, one lady spoke softly in a low voice, "I was also raped but I could not tell my husband." There was silence. Then another one spoke up until five of thirteen women in the group admitted they had been raped.

I asked, "What was done about it?" Nothing! I was told the authorities were no good and they had even laughed at one of the ladies and sent her back home saying it was her fault! I kept praying in my heart about what should we do now. "It is time to act!" was coming to me. The Holy Spirit was convicting me to act. When everyone had a chance to express ideas and opinions, I suddenly remembered I had read a newspaper article not long ago.

There was a rich young man in Quito who drove a red convertible. He was raping nice girls and getting away with it. Five young women devised a plan. They would dress to seduce him and wait by a roadside where they knew he would pass. Soon enough they saw the car coming and he stopped to give them a ride. They looked inside the car and saw sun glasses, scarves and ropes; a few of the items that had been previously reported by some of the victims. It was him.

The most daring of the young women sat in the front seat next to the driver started flirting with him. Soon he stopped in an isolated place and told the others they would have their turn. Yes! The girls knew they would have their turn, just as they had planned. They jumped on him, tied him up securely so he couldn't get away and proceeded to castrate him.

The ladies at the meeting gasped! Then, I replied, "Those young girls were very brave to stop a rapist and protect many other possible victims from this evil man. Here we have the same situation. You have described these men as merchants. They buy cattle at a low price to make money off of the poor.

They are raping the women and no one is stopping them." Now came the big question. "Who would do the castrating?"

Of course they looked at me and said, "You can!" "Oh no," I said.

"I cannot even kill a chicken! Ask my fellow sisters. They will tell you." The sisters who were present supported me.

Then someone said, "Well, as the girls in the newspaper did, we can all do it!" We decided at the morrow we would go to the house of the man who was not far from where we lived and we would talk to him. One of the ladies whispered to me, "Sister, the lady across the room is his mother."

"Oh," I said. "My dear Grandmother, I had no idea we were talking about your son. You will have to come with us for protection."

"Oh no!" she said, looking frightened. "He does not mind me. More than one time he has beaten me when I told him to stop doing the wrong things."

I was horrified. This was a monster we were about to take on. I said, "Ladies, let's remember David and Goliath. " If *God is on our side, who can be against us?"*

We sang to calm our nerves, for we knew the seriousness of what we were about to do. We sang some more and prayed more, and finally went home with the agenda of who was going to do what. The grandma would come but stay in the back with a stick. Another would bring the knife and others the ropes and whatever they thought was necessary for such an operation.

Some of the women had seen and knew how to castrate a pig. We talked of how to bring the man down because he was a big man. He had a wife who never attended the community meetings. She might or might not help. Someone had to take care of the children of the man. "That would be me," I volunteered quickly. I just could not see me watching a man getting castrated. In the group, we never mentioned the secrecy of it all. The sin was public; the abuse had been going on for years. Now it was our time. It was in God's hands. I did not sleep at all even after praying a lot.

The next day when we arrived at the house, everything seemed strange. There were no dogs and no chickens. We knocked at the door. No one answered. We went to a neighbor to ask if he had seen the man of the house. He said, "We heard noises at two in the morning, we saw trucks being loaded and by three a.m. the trucks and everyone left."

Our first reaction was of tremendous joy! We yelled, letting out our fears and realizing God had answered our prayers in the most unexpected way! God's ways are not our ways. God saved us from such an unspeakable way of bringing about justice. We never heard of another incident in that area.

Afterwards, we went to the Commissioner and let him know, what we had almost done because he had been doing nothing. His face turned as white as a sheet and all of his macho bravery with authoritarian voice was gone. It took him a while to recover and tell us that it was dangerous for us to take the law into our own hands.

I said, "There is a higher law than man's law. God does not want this to happen to His daughters. For that we are sure and were about to do it in God's name."

He promised to take better care of victims but excused himself by saying, "I don't have enough policemen to help me." We laughed and said, "That is why we will help!" and left.

At the next community meeting there was much to talk about and celebrate. Our lives as sisters were never boring and we were very happy to be able to help in such a drastic way. It was obvious that God's hand was on us and yet at every turn, we were asked to do more.

Washing neighbors clothes

One time, four of us sisters were going to visit the neighboring community. It was to be a relaxing time to bring food and enjoy the day. We had walked about two blocks and while crossing the bridge, we heard a child crying. It was Imelda a ten-year-old, she was crying near a big pile of dirty laundry at the river bank.

"Let's see what is happening," I said. So we walked down to the water. Imelda explained that her mother had given birth to a new baby and couldn't come to wash the clothes, so she had to wash them. She was so very tired after bringing the clothes to the river and now she had the whole week's dirty laundry to do for the family.

We looked at each other and without a word; we started washing the clothes for her. We hand washed them with a little soap and pressing them against small rocks. It took the four of us women four hours to wash those clothes. Even for me it was overwhelming and to think the child was expected to get this done all by herself. When we finished the washing, we had to carry the very wet and heavy clothes to her home where we draped them on bushes to dry.

The mother was in bed with the newborn baby. We visited a short time and then went home. She was very grateful we had helped her daughter. Everyone found out how the sisters had helped wash the clothes and were very impressed.

It was something totally new to them, to us too! It was evangelizing by example.

About two weeks later, Imelda came to our door asking for help again. I had to sit down with her to explain all the responsibilities we must also do. She would have to tell her mother, she could only do a little at a time, not the whole pile. I suggested she should only bring a small amount of dirty laundry at a time, not the whole pile. She went home a bit sad, yet uplifted. I promised I would talk to her mother and also saw the need to schedule a ladies' meeting soon.

The next day, I made time to go with one of the sisters who would play with the children as I talked to the mother. We had a long visit with her about the problem of expecting the child to do too much, especially since the child must also attend school.

As my mother did, her mother also practiced the custom of taking forty days to recuperate after giving birth and that is why the child had to help. We talked about alternatives, relatives, and friends and came up with a solution.

She would send the girl with her brother to fetch a cousin in the neighboring community to help.

I had more "food for thought" for the ladies' meeting after talking with the mother. It brought up their awareness of how much a child can or cannot be expected to do. I also suggested to the ladies in this rural area that they find alternatives to fall back on, which was helpful to them also.

For those who had been attending the meetings and reading God's Word, it was not hard to be in solidarity and help one another. Those who did not attend the meetings still had to be reached. We had a big job ahead of us. The Christian Community way of evangelizing was being taught and was producing fruit. We felt great about God having taken us down this new road.

Chapter 13

The Earthquake

"Then the disciples came to him and awoke him saying, Lord, save us. We are perishing. But he quieted them, why are you fearful o you of little faith? Then he arose and rebuked the winds and the sea. And there was great calm.

Mat.8-23. (TNAB)

The story I am about to tell took place in Olmedo, Ecuador. I had been selected to conduct a Bible course there. I was delighted to support the Lauritas Sisters. They were very well known; for their compassionate work with the poorest, of the poor in the community.

At this time the COIM group was back in Aguarico but in a different building than when I first lived there. I visited my family on my way to Olmedo. My father and my sister Mercedes were glad I was given this assignment and they wanted to accompany me to Olmedo. It allowed my dad to see where I would be staying. He said: "At least for awhile you will be in a city and giving a Bible course." It is about one and a half hours away from Quito. When he saw the convent, he commented.

"It will be a better place to be; at least they have electricity and running water."

The Spanish-style two-story brick convent building was beside the big church, in the center of the plaza in the city. We arrived about four in the afternoon. In that convent lived five Sisters including the Superior. We talked while having some refreshments. Then my family left with the assurance they would come back to get me after ten days.

The change of climate was very drastic for me. I was used to living in the tropics (hot and humid.) Now I had come to the high mountains, where the coldness goes clear through to the bones.

The Sisters gave me some general information about the people who live there. "We work with the very poor indigenous people. There are also businessmen and affluent people here" were the Sisters' comments. They wanted me to train some leaders on how to evangelize and spread the God Kingdom, through His Word. "There is one important issue here." The Sisters told me.

"This town is supposed to be communist. There are some leaders in town that do not believe in God and we have not been able to reach them." I put that information in the back of my mind to bring it forth when needed.

After we ate, prayed, and had some recreation, the Superior said: "Maria Luisa you must be tired. If you want, you can go to bed." She was right I was tired and cold. I thanked her and expressed my appreciation to all the Sisters for their hospitality along with the promise that the next day we would spend more time; discussing the agenda, answering questions, getting organized and deciding what was most important for them to learn from this Bible study.

I quickly brushed my teeth, washed up, went to bed and promptly fell asleep. It was about 8:30 p.m. March 5, 1987. Around 9:00 p.m. I felt a tremendous shake! I woke up wondering what was going on. There were loud noises in the street, a big light flashed and then just blackness. All the Sisters ran downstairs.

I took my poncho on the way out but as we were going down the steps, the Superior took it from me and here I was just wearing only pajamas in that cold weather.

We sat down to pray and ask God for guidance and help in this time of tribulation. I was so tired I could hardly keep my eyes open. I suggested, "Let's bring the mattresses down to the living room and get some sleep because we have no idea what tomorrow will bring." I lie down and soon fell asleep. The Sisters said, "How can you sleep?" Two Sisters decided to sleep in the car. The others stayed with me in the living room. At 12:00 A.M., I suddenly awakened with a scream. Someone was sleeping on each side of me. It turned out two of the Sisters had joined me and huddled on my mattress after they saw me "sleeping so peacefully," one of them said.

It was as if I were inside a blender. The noise was deafening! I felt the earth shaking up and down, sideways and around! As hard as I tried, I could not stand on my feet. After what seemed like forever, the shaking slowed down and I was able to get on my hands and knees and then I stood up.

The first thing I saw in the corner of the living room was a life-sized statue of Mary on top of a stand which was swaying back and forth rhythmically. I tried to decide whether or not I should get her down so she would not break. Instantly I said, "Mary, you can take care of yourself and don't fall and break." She did not fall nor break.

I rescued my poncho and walked out the door while putting my shoes on. I opened the door and looked out. The sight was something to behold! People from all different directions were coming in rows directly to the convent. All the Sisters were out now. The people right in front of the convent cried, "Sisters help us to pray." I heard the Superior say, "I cannot even breathe much less pray out loud." I piped up, "Sister, I can lead them in prayer." She was glad I volunteered and stayed by my side.

I stood on the steps of the convent to be able to see more, and started telling them the story of the apostles and Jesus in a boat on a lake. When a storm came up, Jesus was sound asleep.

I made a very short reflection, then another small shake came and people screamed. I compared our situation with that of the apostles and suggested. "The next time we get a shake, we must do the same thing the apostles did, call out to Jesus. Let us practice. " I thought if I got them to calling to Jesus, their nerves would calm down and feel better. We practiced calling, "Jesus save us!"

"Louder, louder" I said. Even with all our practice, when the next shake came, everyone screamed. Some remembered to call to Jesus, some just screamed out in fear. There was instant hugging. It did not matter who was around, we just hugged for support. When the shaking stopped one time, I found a twelve year-old boy hanging tightly on to me for dear life. When it subsided, he opened his eyes and was shocked to see it was me he was hugging and not, his mother as he imagined. There was a terrified look on his face. Of course, in those moments you just do what you can. I gave him a smile and a reassuring hug back.

I realized God had given me a great gift. In times of stress and confusion, I come up clear and calm. I praise God for that gift.

After awhile the Doctor of the clinic there, took the initiative and spoke to the people. "If we stay here," he said: "there is the danger of big buildings coming down on us and high voltage electric wires with it. My suggestion is to go to the stadium where we will be safer."

The people agreed and started walking toward the stadium. It was about three blocks from the Convent. Rain was drizzling, *"I wondered if we'd die from the earthquake or catch pneumonia."* The two Sisters, who had gone to be in the car, where my guitar was, came behind us.

When we arrived at the stadium, the doctor spoke again, "The women with babies should be in the center, the rest of the women should stand around them for protection and human warmth, after that the teenagers, and then the young men." Some had brought some plastic and put it on the ground to sit on to keep from getting so wet. They made room for the Sisters. I continued to tell stories of Jesus, prayed the Rosary, and sang playing the guitar.

The Doctor began to organize teams; one to get some old tires to burn for light and warmth, the other to take turns going back to the plaza and policing the unlocked homes in the area to prevent vandalism.

About four in the morning, the Superior told me "You have done enough;" Go to the car to rest and send the Sisters back to take your place. Happily, I accepted and went to the car. In my exhausted sleep, I could feel the rocking of the shakes once in a while. The news from the radio said there had been one thousand small shakes, after the big earthquake from 12:00 a.m. to 5:00 a.m. I slept soundly there in the car until the sun, shining on my face awakened me.

The silence was very much the opposite of what had occurred the night before. Half asleep I looked out and saw a boy taking care of a few sheep at the far end of the stadium. I thought, "I must be dreaming but how do I explain myself being in the middle of the stadium, in a car all by myself?" Then I saw burned tires on the other side. At the same time I heard a knock at the window. A Sister had come and said, "Maria Luisa come and see. The Convent is gone."

We drove to the Convent. It was devastating to realize the beautiful building I had been in the day before was now in rubbles except for two walls. We pushed them with one finger and down they went.

The earth kept shaking so we took turns running in to check out what was left in the convent house to see if we could salvage anything, especially food. We did get some potatoes, onions, beans, salt, sugar, and a couple of pots to cook in. No water of course. We had to search for some and when we found it, we boiled it in a makeshift cooking place on the Convent's backyard.

About seven in the morning, the doctor called a meeting. The decision was to go in pairs to assess the damage, missing, injured, and dead. Also we were to assist those in urgent need in the rural areas. A nurse and I were assigned together. She drove a jeep and we started up to a higher side of the mountain. We stopped at every house on the way to find out how everyone was and to gather statistics.

Mostly the illnesses were caused by nerves and grief over the loss of everything the people owned.

The houses were made of adobe which was flattened by the earthquake. Nothing was left. The family animals had scattered searching for safety. One by one, the animals were found and brought back by their owners.

The third house we stopped at had an urgent situation. The man of the house came running to us as soon as he heard the jeep. Excitedly he said, "My wife is having a baby! We were not expecting the baby for two more months." We went into a dark room where a lady wearing a heavy wool skirt was squatting on the bed. I found out that they give birth by sitting on their heals on the bed.

Remembering what my mother used to do when she helped ladies in these moments, I asked their young six year old son to get some water because there was none around. He had to go a long way and brought back about a liter of water. We needed boiled sterilized water to wash the baby when it arrived. The father went to find wood but it was wet which made it hard to start a fire. It created a lot of smoke. Eventually we succeeded in boiling the water.

Meanwhile the lady was pushing and the baby was coming. I was glad the nurse was there and I felt secure with the thought she could do the hard part and I would just help. When I asked for a knife or scissors to cut the umbilical cord, it was obvious we needed more boiled water to sterilize the knife because the one the man offered was very rusty. I just could not see the nurse cutting the cord with it. The little boy had to make another trip for water.

I asked the father, "Do you have some swaddling clothes to wrap the baby in after it is born?" The lady said, "We were not ready." The father, with looks of panic on his face, stood like a lost soul in the middle of the house. The lady told us where to look. They had a piece of material the size of a typewriter paper.

When the baby was born and we heard his cry, we all felt a great sense of relief. The nurse washed the baby and wrapped him with that piece of material and the mother's old skirt. I wanted to take my blouse off to give it to them. I was so cold; I just could not do it. I prayed God would take care of this family.

I thought of Jesus in the manger. At least he had swaddling clothes ready. This child had nothing to begin with.

The nurse was nervous. She said, "The placenta is not coming." She had been with the mother all this time, guiding her. The nurse said, "The mother was scared and was most grateful we were there to help." We prayed, massaged her stomach and waited.

Later, the nurse told the doctor, "I have helped doctors in the hospital deliver babies but I have never done it by myself in this type of situation." I told them I had seen my mother do it many times. I have no idea how long it took, but we stayed until the placenta came out. Then we left the lady resting peacefully with her son in her arms.

The mayor in the city and all the workers were trying to get the phone lines repaired to be able to communicate with Quito. As soon as I was able to get through, I called my wealthy friends to let them know about the terrible earthquake. The next day school buses came with food and clothing for all.

The family we had helped was very happy, especially the boy. He received a warm jacket and came to show me. The ladies had packed a box just for them with baby clothes and food which I delivered to them. The little boy could not believe it. He kept rubbing the jacket that had a warm lambskin lining.

The best in people came out during this time of need. A couple more stops and we encountered another miracle. We met a lady who said, "My husband is working in Quito and does not know what has happened to us. There is no way to let him know. He does not have a radio and he is working in some faraway place. When the first shake came at nine last night, I brought all the children to my bed to pray. We spent the entire time kneeling down saying one Rosary after another." Of course the little ones probably slept, I used to sleep after saying the Hail Mary twenty times.

She continued, "We asked Our Blessed Mother, to ask Jesus to save us. We have nowhere to go and there will be no help, except from God. When the big 12:00 a.m. earthquake came we prayed louder.

The children and I were very scared but we kept praying and huddling together. The animals had been crying, but there was no way to help them." She decided to stay inside the room and let God take care of them. When morning came, the oldest boys tried to open the door but it was impossible. Finally, making a hole from the inside to get out, one of the small children dug himself out. He yelled, "Mother everything is gone." Then from both sides they tried to open the door to get out. To her great surprise, the room where she was with the children was the only one standing. All the rest of the house was flattened. The animals were gone. She had prayed her husband would come.

When we arrived, he had not come yet. She had started to collect the animals one by one, praising God for the miracle of her life and for sparing her children. No one was hurt and she had just about all the animals tied up again. What an experience. We cried and embraced each other out of joy. We prayed, and let her know we would find a way to communicate with her husband.

Again I could see God's hand in my entire journey. Before I went to the Carmelite Mission, I had the opportunity to work with prosperous members of St. Rafael Church in Quito. I had made a report of the work of all the Parishes for the Archbishop. That is when I met and made friends with some wealthy people. It came in handy now. I knew I could call on them in this catastrophe, because they had previously been generous with their money and means to help the people in the mountains. They were glad to do God's work for the poor.

Now the time came to deliver the food and clothes that were coming in. I had no idea of how to go about it. The doctor put me in charge. "How am I going to do this?" Well, the Holy Spirit helped me; I called on the town leaders to organize the people according to their requested needs. "See how many are in each family. Start with the ones who are in the most need."

It was hard I did not know anyone, but they knew each other. When some of the homeless and mentally disabled were not present, someone would say, "So and so is not here."

We put clothes and food aside until that person showed up. It was wonderful to see the solidarity in them. The so-called Communists disappeared and now everyone acted like believers. Every time there was a bus load of food or clothes, the people would gather around.

We had a room for storage. We needed to start sorting according to the good, the bad and the ugly clothes. We had no extra bags to put the food in. One man came and showed his poncho and said, "Just put everything here. At home we will divide it." We poured the beans, rice, flour, and any other grain there was into the poncho. He was a happy man. All I could think of was how much waste there was in the USA and here we had not one miserable plastic bag to put the food in.

Therefore I say to you, do not worry about your life, what you will eat or what you will drink; or about your body, what you will put on. Is not life more than food and the body more than clothing? Look at the birds of the air, for they neither sow nor reap nor gather into barns; yet your heavenly father feeds them. Are you not of more value than they?

Luke12:24 (TNAB)

I would usually talk about this passage with the people before we distributed the supplies to them. Another well-known passage from the Word of God, I used very much, "We are the Body of Christ." We also sang that as a song. There were so many moments and opportunities now to serve and to talk about God. I did not want to miss any of them. It was a different kind of Bible class God wanted me to give. What started out in our plans as a Bible study, turned out to be a practical application of living like Christ. Not just reading it and studying it.

I had another experience that I feel the need to share, because it is out of the ordinary. There was a young girl, mentally challenged, who could not speak clearly. Everyone in the town knew her.

I asked, "Where does she live." No one knew. I wanted to get to know her. She had seen me and trusted me. When I asked her "Would you take me to the place where you live?"

She told me, "I do not know if the two companions will let me."

I said, "Who are they?"

She said, "I cannot tell you, but I'll ask."

Well she did, and they must have said "yes" because she came back and took hold of my hand and we started walking through some streets. It seemed to me she was lost but I decided to let her lead me. She had the most beautiful smile. She was very innocent. I was told she had no relatives. Finally she led me through an open field. As far as the eye could see there was only grass, no cows. There were signs of cows having been there in the past. We crossed some fences, and then right before a kind of hollow, was the last fence which was hard to cross.

She smiled and said, "My companions' stay here watching to see that no one follows us."

I had not seen anyone but I went along with her. We went down in a kind of a cave. She had fashioned a door with some sticks, logs and cardboards. "Here it is, this is my home," She said There was an old rug for a blanket, one small pot, one spoon, and nothing else. My heart ached when I saw this, yet I saw also how happy she was.

I asked her, "Who are your companions? I did not see them."

She said "I see them all the time. They are angels. Only I can see them. They protect me that I may not get hurt."

I was speechless. I hugged her dearly, she hugged me back tightly. I blessed her and hoped her belief would continue to keep her safe. As a woman, all I could think was, an evil man could follow her, rape her and get her pregnant. I shared this experience with the Sisters and one of my rich lady friends, hoping someone would follow up and help her.

Flying in a cargo plane

My time was up, I was needed urgently back at the mission. The emergency had passed here. I don't remember how I went back to Quito, but I knew I had to change gears. The Ecuadorian Air Force was making regular trips with emergency relief. The German Embassy had given the Church of Sucumbíos a motorcycle for traveling since all the roads were ruined and no cars could drive through. The Bishop told me I had to take it with me. I arrived at the airport just before they finished loading the plane. I pulled in at the gate.

A private whom I had told that I needed to be on that plane said, "You can go in, but no one else."

I asked him and another private who was beside him to help me push the motorcycle into the plane. My brother who was helping me had to stay outside of the gate and watched me. I ran with the privates and the motorcycle and made it into the plane as the back door was closing.

There was much cargo inside. Someone said, "Sister, find a place to sit and hold on!"

I was not interested so much in being buckled up, as I was to see from the window of the plane what damage the earthquake had done. I held onto whatever I could, such as big boxes and bags of food. I found a seat to strap myself into, as the plane took off. I thanked God for the miracle to have made it, onto the plane and for the privates that helped me. I knew there were angels helping me.

Later on I found out that when the Sergeant asked the privates who I was and what permits I had shown for the motorcycle. (see picture #19)

The Sergeant said he would have stopped me, because I had none. My brother overheard the whole conversation. The Sergeant had said, "I will be watching for her next time, because she had no permits. What she did was against the law. She could have caused an incident and also hurt herself." After that I made sure not to fly for a while because my brothers had warned me against it. I remembered how Peter was saved out of jail by angels. I was helped by "two angels" (privates) and arrived safely with the motorcycle, at the church.

I saw overwhelming devastation. Both sides of the river had slid down because of the earthquake. It created a dam, which stopped the river on the south side and caused it to be dry for awhile. The people said they could catch fish with their bare hands by the dozens. No one there knew the river had been dammed up. I could see from the plane the bare sides of the mountains. Then the natural dam that was built with the mud slides broke, it took everything in its path; fields of coffee plantations, banana plantations, homes, animals and people.

The Mission Refugee Center

Upon arriving at the Mission Center with God's help, I felt poorly prepared for what I had to face. The Mission Center had become a refugee camp for all the homeless. There was no water and no electricity. The young people in the COIM group were doing their best trying to find food to feed all these people.

I was totally shocked and surprised to see no progress had been made at repairing the broken water pipes or downed electric poles at the Center. We called a meeting of the missionaries.

The Principal of the College and the Director of the Boarding school, Brother Gonzales said, "We can have water in three days if we can get pipes. We have asked for them, but we get no answer."

I said, "You have the authority to close the College and the Boarding school. Why don't you use it? We are about to have a disaster here. People are becoming feverish. We can't have two hundred people with no water! All the bushes around are full of mosquitoes. We will have an epidemic on our hands!"

I told the secretary on the radio. "I need to speak with the Bishop,"

She said, "He is in a meeting."

"All right" I said. "Take a note and give it to him exactly as I say. If he doesn't send 300 meters of pipe today, we will close the Boarding School, and the College. We will send the people, who are using the Center as a shelter, to wherever we can. We won't be responsible for the epidemic that surely will come."

That same day at 3:00 p.m. the first plane arrived from Quito. A priest came with the water pipes. I told Brother Miguel, "Here are your pipes;" I need the water and electricity yesterday." This did not help my reputation of being a bossy, domineering woman who takes over.

Everyone did the best they could under the circumstances. Each missionary had been assigned to their own ministry, but the earthquake just turned the plans upside down.

In the meantime, I started learning which people were there for shelter and which ones had a family to go to. I found out some children were truly orphans. There was no one who would be asking for them.

An Orphan finds a Relative

Every missionary was helping. One time we could not get any information from a seven year old. A priest was appointed to take her to an orphanage in Quito. As they were waiting at the airport, a lady came close to them and recognized and talked to the little girl. She said, "I was her teacher last year and know her parents." We stopped the process. Thank God we had someone that knew her. It was another miracle. It was painful to even think what this little girl would have suffered had she been lost in the shuffle.

The children that were a little older could tell us, about their families in other towns. We were able to get them reunited. At first we could not find the family of a child. Finally we found an aunt. Her parents had died when the dam burst.

Little by little, as we were getting things in order, there were fewer people stranded at the Mission Center.

In order to visit the communities we used the motorcycle, as there was no way a car could get through the roads. I asked Gribaldo, one of the young men in the group to teach me how to drive the motorcycle. Soon I realized that it was too stressful for me and it would be better for him to take me around.

There was a young teenage boy who saw his whole family float away in the angry river. His parents told him to climb the biggest tree he could find and he obeyed. He kept climbing until he couldn't climb anymore. He said he hung on to a branch the whole night, until the river went down. When he saw it was safe, he got down to look for his home. Everything they owned was gone. The river had taken a different course and his family's land was in the middle of it. He was left with nothing, even no relatives.

Every missionary was involved in the people's lives. The pain was only lessened by their hope in Jesus Christ and the courage that came from Him.

So many times I asked Jesus to calm the storm inside me and He did. Things were never the same at the Mission.

It took a very long time to feel a sense of normalcy. The personal stories and experiences after the earthquake were many; some horrific and others miraculous. At the community meetings the subject of the earthquake came up for a long time. We all needed to mourn, for what was and is no more. It was very painful. We all needed time to let go of the losses and everyone had to find their own way. The most important help was Jesus Christ and the Word of God which gave us strength and hope and courage in these times.

Chapter 14

Growing Pains and Moving On

"The way we came to know love was that He laid down his life for us; so, we ought to lay down our lives for our brothers."

1 John 4: 16 (TNAB)

As the group was growing, the time came to divide into two groups. Some of us would stay at San Vicente and others would go to ISAMIS Aguarico Center. I went to the Mission Center with Mary, Grivaldo, Pablo, Macario, and Flor. The rest of the group would stay at San Vicente with Elida as the Coordinator.

Mary goes to College

Mary was attending evening classes at the College; I usually drop her, and pick her up at the bus stop in the city. One night it was pouring rain, while I was waiting for the bus. I was wearing a rain poncho with a hood. I stood by a wall of the building when two men came towards me one from each side. It was a dangerous area. I planted my feet, cross my arms and was getting prepare to fight. The men kept pressing closer and closer, I could feel their breath and body warmth.

I did not want to open my mouth, to let them know I was a woman. I prayed to God to come to my aid. Just when it seemed both men were about to get me, the bus lights flashed on. The men ran away.

Mary told me, the bus was late because of a problem. I was trembling. I realized one more time, we have God on our side, and nothing or no one could harm us. I could not help but be concerned about Mary, when she was going to study, but I trust in the Lord that she would be safe.

Reverend Arroyo was building a minor ISAMIS Seminary. It was located across a small creek in the back of the students' dormitories. The site caused a hardship in transporting materials down then up a hill. Yet, with much effort, good direction and hard work, the U shaped building was completed. On one side was the ladies dormitory, across from it was the men's dormitory. A big lawn separated the two. Where the U connected each side there was a kitchen, dining room and classrooms at the front.

The surroundings needed to be cleared of underbrush. The young men were glad to get their muscles to work cutting the trees and clearing all around the place for a future garden. We wanted to make sure snakes or animals could not find a place to make their homes.

This was a different living situation, compared to the ones we had lived in before as a group. Now we had running water and electricity. We would take a full week each month for intense studies. The Missionary teachers from Pacifico Zambrano College would be the regular instructors and I taught Christology and Evangelization.

The communities of Via Coca would be our task. The administration of the center and hospitality to the missionaries were part of our responsibilities, along with taking care of the formation center for all the lay ISAMIS leaders. A very spacious octagon-shaped building made of concrete blocks was used for reunions and conferences. Some offices and bathrooms were on the side of the building.

Celso, my brother came with his family to help at the mission. During this time, my brother and his family stayed at the two-story building which was the Bishop's residence.

Celso's daughter Katita remembers how she climbed the steps and looked down at the Aguarico River from the terrace. It was a big change from the earlier visit at San Vicente. They were better able to enjoy the stay and scenery because of the modern living accommodations.

Celso is a teacher and very artistic. He sketched on the front wall the goal of ISAMIS. It had been chosen after much deliberation by the Missionary Assembly: "The holistic liberation of man from the poor for the cause of the Kingdom. *"Liberación integral del hombre desde los pobres por la causa del Reino*. The family stayed as Celso completed the different designs with macramé of colored-yarn at the window openings. It certainly gave a creative and inspiring look to the conference area. There were many appreciative comments after it was completed. He had obviously planted a seed in the ISAMIS with his God-given talent...(see picture #20)

I was always pleased with him but now I was especially grateful for his talent, in making a meaningful contribution to the beauty of the conference center. As soon as anyone sat down, they could see the words right in front of them. The message was clear. The peasants, indigenous people and leaders of the communities enjoyed it very much. It was a good reminder of why we were there: "It was for the cause of the Kingdom of God."

The youth, a blessing for the Mission

The year 1987 was very eventful. The earthquake happened, Macario was sent to Panama for training, Noemi to Central America, and Jose to Peru. Edgar received the Sacrament of Holy Orders from Bishop Gonzalo. He was the first ordained Ecuadorian priest from and for ISAMIS. It was the realization of one of Gonzalo's dreams. It was one more step in building the local Church...(see picture #21)

There were some memorable moments with the group. One of them was on my birthday. We celebrated everybody's birthday in a simple but meaningful way. At one of those celebrations for my birthday, the young members serenaded me.

According to Macario, they were very surprised when I came out with sweet biscuits for them and had an early party right then and there.

On some of the evenings when the opportunity allowed and all our responsibilities had been taken care of, we would plan some kind of recreation. We played cards, sang songs, or recited poems. Other times we danced, remembering King David danced in front of the Ark. We would also pick a tune and while I played the guitar, each one as the spirit moved them would spontaneously add a verse. We had a good time. I was always amazed and inspired by these young people; who were able to invent all kinds of simple ways to enjoy life and be happy about every seemingly small thing that came their way. We lived every day as if it were the last day of our lives...(see picture #22)

Suffering for the kingdom

I thanked God for each one who came and lived among us. They showed in many ways how much they cared for me. However, my health was gradually getting worse.

While visiting one of the families in this area, I experienced more than once the enemies of the jungle, the parasites. This family I was visiting lived on a hill which was not easy to get to. Coffee plants were all around the house. There was not much open space. I could see they had a couple of pigs, two dogs, and chickens. They had lived there for a long time. I was welcomed to their home and offered lemonade. I chose to sit on the hammock and hold the baby.

I noticed that everyone there, the lady of the house and the children, were scratching. At that time I did not think much about it. We drank the lemonade they offered, talked and listened to how they were doing. I reminded them of the importance of attending the meeting when the missionaries visited the community. We prayed for their personal needs and left.

I arrived home, a couple of hours later, I started itching. The itching became unbearable so I went to the Mission Clinic. As soon as Sister Carmen saw me, she said she knew what it was. It was a bug that gets under the skin and travels all over.

She was alarmed for the family also. She said, "The house has to be infested. You must send someone to tell them to come and see me. They will have to burn everything they have. There is no other way."

Everything I touched had to be burned. I was kept at the clinic for a day. Sister Carmen covered me with a cream from head to toe. I do not remember how long it took to feel better. I did send a message to the family so they'd know what they were up against. They did not know what to do about their problem. I was told they did burn the house and all their belongings.

I asked Abram, who took care of the storage room, to give the people anything they could use from the supplies we had. We had extra beds from the boarding school and clothes we received from the United States for the poor. I thanked God for the ability to help them. I saw how many people suffer in silence and take it as a part of life without complaint. I was sent there for a reason.

I was happy to help even though I had to go through this infection myself. I realized, that was what Jesus did.

He became one of us and took on our sins. I took this "family bug" with me to be able to help them. Months later the family came to thank me and told me how they had that itching for such a long time. The mother had been praying and asking for help. It was God's answer for them that we went to visit.

During this time, peasants visited the Center asking for help. I was thankful I could help and had the means and authority to do it. The reward was great as I heard their appreciative words and receive their signs of affection and love.

One of those people was the lady with the miracle baby. One day she came and brought me a gold nugget. I did not want to accept it. I told her she could sell it and buy clothes for her children. She said she does that with other nuggets but this one was for me because they had seen my love for them. For a long time I kept it as a remembrance of her but in the process of all my travels, I misplaced it. Yet the memory of her never fades.

Another time, a Quechua man called Antonio brought me a snake skin. He said if I ever go back to the United States, to take it to remember them. It was difficult to take their gifts but I learned it made them happy, not to be only on the receiving end. God's people are so wonderful and awesome. I saw the happiness the Word of God brought to them. No suffering was too much for the sake of the Kingdom.

At one of our Christmas celebrations, we had a Christmas Carol competition. As a group we sang "Silent Night." The verses I sang in English and the chorus we all sang in Spanish. The judges loved it and gave us first prize. I loved working with the youth. Their enthusiasm, energy, dedication and love of God were very appealing to me. We put on Christmas pageants puppet shows with the different groups.

At Easter time we enacted the passion of Jesus. This was very special to them. It made a great impact on the people. There were many different ways we used to plant the Word of God in their hearts. It was very rewarding even though my health was continuing to decline.

It did not matter if I had to spend time and energy. I felt if God wanted me to do this, He would supply the strength and of course. He always did!

Domestic violence

One morning while I was busy taking care of business, a woman came asking for me. When I went to see her, it was a shocking sight. She was so dirty! Her sunken eyes told me of her lack of sleep. Her hair was messy, in dire need of a comb, shampoo and water. Her bloody face and black eye told me the seriousness of the visit. I gasped, said a short silent prayer and went to her with open arms asking, "What happened?" She lifted her hand to wipe tears from her face and started sobbing aloud. Her body was shaking as I held her and I felt as if she were going to faint. I found a chair so she could sit and calm down until she was able to tell me what happened.

I gave her a glass of water and asked the Sisters to prepare her some food and find clothes for her because what she was wearing was torn, dirty and bloody. I guessed she had not eaten for some time. Finally after a drinking some water, she became calmer and between sobs, told me her story.

By this time I realized how common these sad experiences were for women like her in these places. She was alone and had no relatives nearby. Her husband brought her from Loja.

She said, "He drinks a lot, and his jealousy overtakes him and he becomes like the devil." She described his behavior saying, "It does not matter what I do or don't do. He finds any excuse to hit me until I pass out or until he gets tired and falls asleep. I have no one to turn to. The neighbors are too far away and he promised me if I ever left him, he would kill me.

I heard about you missionaries. Please help me."

She continued, "Yesterday he came back from Lago Agrio. He had spent all the money that he received from selling the coffee, which both of us worked for. He did not buy any food for the week. All I did was to ask him, how are we going to survive this coming week? We have no food, no salt, no sugar, and no soap. How am I going to wash your clothes?

He became very angry and started beating me. For the first time, I tried to fight back, but he is big and strong. I took a stick and hit him. We struggled. The only thing in my favor was that he was very drunk, he kept falling down. But he got up grabbing me, and that is why my dress is torn."

She showed me the scars under her clothes, and black and blue marks all over. She said, "I decided to leave him, when he finally fell down and did not get up again." She walked all night through the jungle, hiding and hoping no one would see her. The scenario was unimaginable, unthinkable, and horrifying to me. "He knows you are the only person I would come to ask for help. He may come here when he wakes up and does not find me," she said.

The Sisters brought the food to her. She started eating. That gave me a chance to get on the radio to call Reverend Arroyo to come and help in case her husband arrived with a rifle. After assessing the situation, I talked to the other missionaries to see what we could do to help her. She gratefully took the clothes and went to take a shower.

I showed her a bed where she could rest and assured her, we were going to have a plan soon. An hour later, I went to check on her and she was fast asleep.

As a group and with Reverend Arroyo's help, we came up with a suggestion. Going to the authorities was not an option. We had seen what they do. They listen, give a pat on the shoulder, and would tell her to go back home because that is her duty as a wife. The abuser is told to stop and then they let him go. Of course he promises to stop, apologizes and asks for forgiveness. Then he does it again the next time he gets drunk.

It was up to us missionaries to help her. She was in danger of losing her life. She did not want to go back to her husband. "He has done this many times," She repeated.

Our suggestion was that she could go to Quito with one of us accompanying her and would stay at the Carmelite place, "El Jordan." She could help in the kitchen until she was able to contact her family in Loja and go back to them. Her face lit up and she was able to crack a smile. She thanked every one of us with a hug and tears. I had to hold back my tears at these times.

We let the team in Quito know of the situation. They agreed to welcome her and help her continue on her journey. The Sisters also prepared a small bag for her with more changes of clothes. I always had a good feeling after we helped someone. As a group we thanked God for what we were able to do.

We ask for His protection and preparedness for whatever was to come in the future. At times I felt helpless because I thought of the many more, we could not help. The thought was overwhelming.

A daughter is given away

Another incident happened when a teenager came one morning to talk to me. I was surprised to see her so early. She told me, "Sister, you have to help me. My mother has given me to an old man! She says she cannot feed all of us children alone and I am 13 years old. She says he is rich and can take care of me. For her, it will be one less mouth to feed; my helping her at home is not enough. She says. I can help her by going away with this ugly old man. I am afraid of him. My mom told me I have to sleep with him. I do not want to! So I came to ask you to help me."

I asked, "Do you have any relatives, like uncles, aunts, grandparents, anyone else? And if so, where do they live?" She remembered that she did have some relatives but, she was not sure they would want her. We talked some more, seeking a solution.

Another Sister and I went to talk to her mother to see what we could do. The mother was definitely not happy that the daughter came to us for help. It was time to give this mother some different ideas. We talked about God, the community meetings, and the help she could get through them. Her solution was not a good one for the girl.

She listened for a long time then she spoke again. She said, "I am afraid someone will take advantage of the girl and she will get pregnant and bring in another mouth to feed." She was desperate and just could not do it by herself. Her husband had run off with a younger woman. Then she said, "If you Sisters go and talk to my sister Claudia, who has no children and is better off, she may take her in." This was a good solution.

The mother agreed to come to the Center when she was desperate and to attend the community meetings, to become a member of the group. She collected the girl's belongings and gave them to me in a plastic bag. We ended the visit praying and thanking God for His mercy.

I went back to talk to the girl. The young Sisters had been taken care of her and she was talking to them. When I told her about our conversation with her mother, her face lit up. She was delighted and relieved. So we planned our trip. We had to leave our present agenda for another day and go with what had walked into our lives. It was another divine interruption, which we had become so familiar with. *Not my will but thine, oh Lord.*

We arrived at the aunt's house in the middle of the afternoon. She was surprised to see us with her niece. She immediately asked, "What has happened? Is my sister all right?"

We responded. "Don't worry, she is all right, but needs your help."

The other Sister took the girl to look at the house while I talked to the aunt. When she heard the story, she was surprised and sorry. She told me, "I would have helped my sister sooner had I known the need. Of course, I will take the girl in. I will be glad to have a companion. I live close to the school and will register her there. I did not finish elementary school and I want her to be able to finish it."

We had already talked to the girl and knew she wanted to come and be with her aunt. When we called her in, she acted a little shy but was smiling. The aunt opened her arms and hugged her. We prayed together, thanking God for His love and mercy. I also thanked the aunt and promised I would keep in touch to see how they were getting along.

She said, "My husband will be happy because he has been concerned that when he goes to work there is no one else with me at home. Now I have the solution. I am sure he will approve."

I told her, "I know this is how God works for good for all those who love Him."

We went back home relieved and grateful to have experienced another of God's miracles. Every step of the way He sent us angels, disguised as ordinary people to help us when we seemed unable to find a solution.

My health was getting worse. The Doctor told me bluntly, "If you do not get out of here and stay away, I give you three months to live. You have to stop this type of life."

I had given all I had. I was worn out but happy. I knew for certain I was doing God's will. I thought if it was my time to die, I was ready. It was for a good cause. I wrote to my friends in the USA. I talked to my family. Everyone advised me to leave. My job was finished and from all the poor health signs, I had to give up and find another way to serve God.

God spoke to me through Louise Burgan and her father who found the answer for me through a scholarship from the Sisters of St. Joseph of Orange at the University of Berkeley Graduate Theological Union in California. I was constantly asking God's guidance. All I wanted was to do His will. Now it seem my work at the Mission was over. I must go on.

It was very difficult to tell the other members of the group about my decision to leave. One by one, I explained how I saw my work was completed here. All I wanted to do was God's will.

They had seen my health deteriorate and knew what the doctor had advised. Even though they understood, their reactions broke my heart. Macario wrote. "Maria Luisa left us as orphans." We had been so close. The others expressed how much the training had helped them to grow as people, to understand life, to know God in another dimension and to deepen their spirituality.

I wrote to accept the scholarship to the Graduate Theological Union in Berkeley. California, USA. My last night at the mission we had a very nice dinner, we talked and sang and the last song was dedicated to me. The words are:

You are going, but you leave behind the trees that you planted. Someone will water them and they will grow.

I took a few small souvenirs from Ecuador for the friends in the USA that had kept in contact with me during those years as a missionary. Again I left everything to begin the new chapter in my life in Berkeley, California.

My friends Rose and Elaine were waiting for me at the airport. The next day, they took me shopping for clothes. I would be going to the university, and they were very generously preparing me and took care of all my needs. I am forever grateful. I continue to see the love and power of God woven in my life and the lives of all the people I ministered to I praise Him love Him and Thank Him constantly.

These are just some of the experiences while I ministered in Ecuador, as I saw the hand of God at work. I tried to select the most interesting events to share with you. My hope and deep desire are that you too would go on to follow God's leading in your life and see miracles unfold on your journey.

Resources

The New American Bible (TNAB)

Vatican Council II The Conciliar and Post Conciliar Documents 1992

The Power of the Poor in History by Reverend Gustavo Gutierrez 1983

Sucumbíos de la Misión Carmelita a la Iglesia Local II by: Luciano Luis Luis.1970-1995

First draft Ladies Vocational Group 1982

COIM Pamphlets 1982-1987

Personal notes from Macario Castillo Peña 1987-2009

Letters from Elida Jimenez 1986-2009

Letters from Mery Rumipamba 1986-2009

Historical Notes from Maria Luisa Jimenez 1980- 1987

Endnotes

1 Sucumbíos de la Misión Carmelita a la Iglesia local, Luciano Luis Luis, pg.266 "La X ASAMBLEA

2 Evangelic Nuntianti, Pope Paúl V

3 Sucumbíos de La Misión Carmelita a la Iglesia local by: Luciano Luis Luis, 1995 serie histórica)

4 The forming of a Community thesis and Project Report of Louise Burgan, BSW candidate of master degree 1981

5 The forming of a Community thesis and Project Report of Louise Burgan, BSW candidate of master degree 1981

6 The forming of a Community thesis and Project Report of Louise Burgan, BSW candidate of master degree 1981

7 Sucumbíos de La Misión Carmelita a la Iglesia local by: Luciano Luis Luis, 1995 serie histórica)

8 Sucumbíos de La Misión Carmelita a la Iglesia local by: Luciano Luis Luis, 1995 serie histórica pg. 55

Sucumbíos de La Misión Carmelita a la Iglesia local by: Luciano Luis Luis, 1995 serie histórica, pg 57-65-68-364

Macario wrote

According to Elida

www.ingramcontent.com/pod-product-compliance
Lightning Source LLC
LaVergne TN
LVHW010202070526
838199LV00062B/4464